Tastes & Tales
along the
Tunnel of Trees

A sweet and savory celebration of
recipes and remembrances along
Historic Michigan Highway M-119

Cover Photo
Lake Shore Drive, 1950 by Virgil D. Haynes.
© Haynes Studio, Harbor Springs

Illustrations by
Jane Cardinal

Published by
The Friends of the Readmond, Friendship and Cross Village
Volunteer Fire & Rescue Squad

Printed and bound in the United States of America by Gilson Graphics, Grand Rapids, Michigan.

Second printing, October 2013

ISBN 978-0-615-80505-4

For the Readmond – Friendship – Cross Village Volunteer Fire and Rescue Squad

… We dedicate this community cookbook to the Firefighters and First Responders who volunteer their time, talent and expertise to keep our rural townships safe.

… We honor and thank these men and women who protect our homes and our lives.

Table of Contents

Readmond – Friendship – Cross Village Volunteer Fire and Rescue

In the late 1970s, concerned residents and property owners in Readmond and Friendship Townships of northern Michigan's Emmet County banded together to solve the problem of long response times to fires and medical emergencies. A group worked to secure property for a fire station, funds for equipment, and volunteers to serve as firefighters and rescue personnel.

In order to supplement individual donations, they started a Mini Fair in Good Hart with proceeds supplying funds to purchase used equipment and to start a fire department from scratch. The Johnston family, early area settlers, donated land on Robinson Road for a fire hall and members and supporters built the building. Soon Cross Village Township joined the effort and the Readmond, Friendship, Cross Village Fire Department, now known as R.F.C. Fire and Rescue, was underway.

The annual Mini Fair continues to contribute to the support of the squad financially and it has been a catalyst for building a spirit of community in the area. Today the squad is a progressive, dynamic organization continually adapting to meet the increasing demands of a growing year-round population and the seasonal addition of thousands of tourists and visitors to the area. A separate training fund allows the squad to offer professional training to all volunteer firefighters and first responders.

These volunteers not only put out fires; they rescue snowmobilers in deep inland forests, collaborate with the U.S. Coast Guard and local agencies to search for and save victims of water accidents in Lake Michigan, aid people involved in motorcycle, automobile and bicycle accidents, and support families having medical emergencies in their homes, cottages and cabins. These trained volunteers leave their jobs during the day, get up from their beds in the middle of the night, attend weekly training sessions and respond quickly and expertly to emergencies throughout a geographic area which includes over 26 miles of Lake Michigan shoreline and thousands of acres of inland farms, hills and forests.

If you live in the area, please consider volunteering for the fire and/or rescue service. Call the fire department office at 231-526-2565 or visit www.rfcfirerescue.org for more information.

DRIVE – HARBOR SPRINGS

The Friends of the Readmond, Friendship
and Cross Village Fire and Rescue Squad
Gratefully acknowledges the following
Cookbook Sponsors

Chief

The Patti Allerding Memorial Fund provided initial seed money for the cookbook and its publication.

Assistant Chief

Jim and Patricia Clarke
Robert and Susan Clarke
Mary M. Schubert, President – Chippewa Cove

Fire Fighter, First Responder

Sally and Ian Bund
Deborah Dicken
Al Dicken – Northern Rock LLC
Trina and Larry Hayes
Dick and Gail Selvala
Dave and Carolyn Shear
Anonymous

Petoskey-Harbor Springs Area
community foundation

**With support from the Community Endowment Fund
and the Baiardi Family Foundation Fund in the Petoskey-
Harbor Springs Area Community Foundation**

RFC Friend

Meeyung and Robert Ainsworth
Patti and Allan Allerding
American Spoon Foods
Jim and Beata Bacus
Linda and Rick Bolton
The Crooked Tree Book Co., LLC – Jane Cardinal, Connie Cobb
John and Nona Carr
Susan Sparrow Carson
Joan Chapman
Joan and Roger Craton
Christopher and Carolyn Dettmer
Hadley and Ethan Dettmer & family
First Community Bank
David and Vicki Fuger
Rick and Carol Godfrey
Graham Real Estate – Good Hart and Harbor Springs
Gurney's Bottle Shop
Jim and Janie Hess
Suzanne and Dennis Hug
Irish Boat Shop, Inc.
Sally and Ken Kelsey
Sara Latimer
Bill and Linda Little
Litzenburger Landscape
MacGregor Plumbing and Heating
Maureen Neff Mayne
Mary Beth Mellen
Chuck Otis
Suzy Parson
Primitive Images – Ceci Bauer
Richner & Richner, LLC
Del and Mary Rigby
Joe and Gail Tomlinson
MaryAnn and Michael VanLokeren
Tom and Nancy Whittingham
Dr. and Mrs. Philip Woollcott
Anonymous

SHORE DRIVE

A hearty thank you to our contributors for your wonderful recipes, pictures and stories. You have helped make this a memorable book.

We thank Cynthia Haynes for permission to use the 1950s era Virgil D. Haynes Photographic Images.

We thank Rosemary V.B. Stolt for permission to use her drawings.

A special thank you to graphic artist Cyndy Shaw of Shaw and Company for her expert advice, design assistance and digital implementation of the cookbook.

The Cookbook Committee

Patricia Clarke and Trina Hayes, Co-Editors

Jane Cardinal, Illustrator and Graphic Design Layout

Patti Allerding

Debbie Dicken

Sally Kelsey

Linda Little

Mary Rigby

Carolyn Shear

The Cookbook Committee dedicates our work to the memory of our friend and colleague, Patti Allerding.

Appetizers

St. Ignatius Church, Middle Village, 1950s, by Virgil D. Haynes
©Haynes Studio, Harbor Springs

Recipes

Savory Spinach Balls

MAKES 30 BALLS

Have this recipe on hand for unexpected guests or to take to someone. It came from my grandson's preschool cookbook and he is now 24! It's been a hit with everyone I've served them to and that's a lot of people. It seems that most people really do like spinach.

1 10-ounce package frozen chopped spinach, cooked and drained well

2 large eggs, slightly beaten

6 tablespoons melted butter or margarine

1 cup Pepperidge Farm Herb Dressing, crushed to crumb texture

1/2 cup grated Parmesan cheese

1/2 medium mild onion, chopped finely

- Preheat oven to 350^0.
- Mix ingredients together until well mixed. Make small balls. Place on non-stick cookie sheets (or lightly greased regular sheets).
- Bake for 15 minutes.
- Make a double batch as they freeze well. If you wish to freeze the spinach balls, do so *before* baking them. Chill them on a cookie sheet until they are firm (either in the refrigerator or freezer).
- Then place them in freezer bags and freeze.
- Defrost desired amount before baking for 15 minutes.

Mary Beth Mellen

Stuffed Mushrooms

1 3-ounce package cream cheese
1 4-ounce package crumbled blue cheese
2 tablespoons mayonnaise
4 slices bacon, cooked, drained and crumbled
1 pound mushroom caps

- Mix cream cheese, crumbled blue cheese, mayonnaise and crumbled bacon.
- Fill mushroom caps with cream cheese mixture. Place caps on a lightly greased cookie sheet. Refrigerate.
- Shortly before serving, preheat oven to 450°.
- Bake for 10 minutes.

Sally Kelsey

A pioneer Michigan pathway

Cowboy Caviar

1 15-ounce can shoepeg corn, drained
1 can black eyed peas, drained
2 avocados, cubed
2/3 cup cilantro, chopped
2/3 cup green onions, chopped
1/2 cup tomatoes, chopped

DRESSING:
1/4 cup olive oil
1/4 cup red wine vinegar
2 garlic cloves, minced
3/4 teaspoon salt
1/8 teaspoon pepper
1 teaspoon cumin

- Combine corn, peas, avocados, cilantro, green onion and tomatoes in a large bowl.
- Mix the dressing ingredients together, then add to the vegetable mixture and stir.
- Refrigerate. Make a few hours before serving to allow the flavors to combine.
- Serve with tortilla chips.

Lindsey Pfaff

Shoepeg Corn

The name "shoepeg corn" derives from a shoemaking term used during the 1800s. Shoepeg corn kernels resemble the wooden pegs used to attach soles to the upper part of shoes.

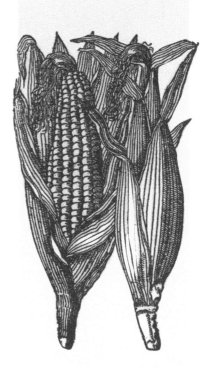

Antipasto Cocktail Relish

This recipe has been a family tradition for over 40 years. One of Lafayette, Indiana's best cooks shared it with me and it's required that it be ready when family arrives for vacation in the summer or at Christmas. Since it keeps well, it also makes a great gift when packed in a jar and taken to a neighbor who has company.

1 12-ounce bottle chili sauce
1 12-ounce bottle hot catsup or regular catsup with a
   dash of Tabasco Sauce
1 6-ounce can tomato paste
1 8-ounce can mushrooms, stems and pieces, drained
1 12-ounce can white chunk tuna, drained
1 16-ounce bag cooked shrimp, defrosted
1 8-ounce jar sweet pickle relish
1 5¾-ounce can chopped ripe pitted olives, drained
1½ tablespoons Worcestershire Sauce

- Mix all ingredients together.
- Serve with Ritz crackers.
- This mix keeps for 2 weeks in the refrigerator.

Trina Hayes

Five-Fruit Salsa

2 cups chopped cantaloupe
6 green onions, chopped
3 kiwi fruit, peeled and chopped
1 navel orange, peeled and chopped
1 sweet yellow pepper, seeded and chopped
1 sweet red pepper, seeded and chopped
1 8-ounce can unsweetened pineapple, drained
2 jalapeno peppers, seeded and finely chopped
1 cup fresh strawberries, hulled and chopped

- Mix all ingredients together except strawberries and let sit to develop flavors.
- Just before serving, add the strawberries.
- Serve with chips.

Sharon Spencer,
Pond Hill Farm

The original altar at Holy Cross Church, Cross Village

Easy Cheesy Buffalo Chicken Dip

SERVES 20

We moved from Saginaw to Cross Village over 20 years ago and weekends were for parties at the beach and for welcoming family and friends. Football season meant tailgate parties. This was a favorite whatever the occasion.

1 8-ounce package cream cheese, cubed
1½ cups cooked chicken, finely chopped
1/2 cup Kraft Roka Blue Cheese Dressing
1/2 cup Buffalo Wing Sauce
2 stalks celery, finely chopped

- Mix all ingredients in a medium-sized microwavable bowl.

- Cook in the microwave oven on high for 5 minutes or until the cream cheese melts. and the mixture is heated through, stirring after 3 minutes.

- Serve hot with crackers or celery stalks.

Sue Parson

Hot Artichoke Dip

SERVES 6
1 14-ounce can artichoke hearts, drained and chopped
1 cup Hellmann's mayonnaise
1 cup Parmesan cheese, grated
Garlic powder to taste

- Preheat oven to 350^0.
- Mix all ingredients and place in an ovenproof ramekin suitable for serving.
- Bake for 20 minutes until mixture bubbles.
- Serve with crackers.

Susan Thomas

**Blisswood
Resort**

Five Generations in Good Hart

Susan's mother, Virginia Thomas, known as Mom Tom, came with her family to the area known as Blisswood by stagecoach from Harbor Springs in 1910. It's now the Thomas family's fifth generation enjoying summers in Good Hart.

"Mother loved going out to dinner but during her last summer that was not possible. Quite often I fixed this favorite treat that she enjoyed. You may also add spinach or water chestnuts for a variation."

Northern Michigan Curry Dip

1 cup mayonnaise
1 teaspoon curry
1 teaspoon horseradish
1 teaspoon dried minced onion
1 teaspoon cider vinegar
1 teaspoon prepared mustard

- Mix all ingredients together and refrigerate for at least 2 hours to blend the flavors.
- Serve with fresh vegetables.

Trina Hayes

Crab Dip

1 8-ounce package cream cheese, softened
1 – 2 cloves garlic, freshly pressed
1 tablespoon dill
1/4 cup mayonnaise
1 teaspoon lemon juice
Crab meat (4 – 6 ounces), flaked
1/2 cup mozzarella cheese, shredded
1 – 2 green onions, sliced
1 Roma tomato, diced (optional)

- Mix the first 5 ingredients and spread on a serving plate or in a pie or tart dish.
- Liberally sprinkle crab meat over the cheese mixture.
- Top with shredded mozzarella cheese then with sliced green onions and diced tomato for a dash of color and flavor.
- Serve with pita chips or your favorite cracker.

Laura Ward

Nan Vincent's Cheese 'N Crab Dip

1 stick butter
1 package imitation crab
1 jar Old English Cheese Spread
1 teaspoon lemon juice
Worcestershire Sauce, a dash

- Preheat oven to 350^0.
- Melt butter in a medium saucepan.
- Add imitation crab, cheese spread, lemon juice and Worcestershire Sauce.
- Bake until cheese melts.

Nan Vincent
from Carolyn Sutherland

The Good Hart Store from years past

Crab Artichoke Casserole Dip

3 tablespoons flour
3 tablespoons butter
1½ cups milk
1 teaspoon salt
1/4 teaspoon Worcestershire Sauce
1/4 teaspoon pepper
2 cups crab meat
4 eggs, hard cooked, quartered
1 16-ounce can artichoke hearts, drained
1/3 cup Parmesan cheese, grated

- Preheat oven to 350°.
- Make a cream sauce by combining the flour, butter, milk, salt, Worcestershire Sauce and pepper in a medium sauce pan over low heat until mixed well.
- Add crab meat to cream sauce.
- Place quartered eggs in the bottom of a 1½ quart casserole dish. Top with drained artichoke hearts and crab meat cream sauce. Sprinkle with Parmesan cheese.
- Bake for 30 minutes.
- Serve with bread, toast rounds or crackers.

Marti Wallen

Cross Village or La Croix

When explorers first landed at Cross Village, they erected a large cedar cross on the bluff above the shore side settlement. The Native Americans asked that the cross be placed over the burial site of a beloved chief. Many subsequent crosses have replaced the first cross. The Odawa word for the village became A-na-mi-a-wa-tig-on-ing or "place by the prayer tree."

Myrt and Sam Johnston

Chicken Liver Paté

MAKES 1½ CUPS

My family, "the Johnston family," has had a farm in Good Hart on Robinson Road since 1934. Besides raising cattle and crops we always had chickens. This recipe was a good way to deal with all those livers and it was yummy, too! Sam and Myrtle Johnston donated the land for the RFC Fire Hall on Robinson Road.

1 medium onion, quartered
1/2 pound chicken livers
4 tablespoons chicken fat, melted
2 hard-cooked eggs, separating yolks from whites
1 teaspoon salt
1/2 teaspoon pepper
1 tablespoon red wine

- Sauté onions and livers in chicken fat until tender.
- Put livers, onions and egg whites through a grinder or grind in a food processor.
- Add seasonings and wine and mix well to form a smooth paste.
- Chop egg yolks and use for garnish.
- Serve on your favorite crackers or toast rounds.

Dixie Ira

Dave's Paté

1 pound Braunschweiger, diced
2 cloves garlic, mashed
1/2 teaspoon sweet basil
1 medium onion, minced

- Beat well with an electric mixer and mold into a ball. Place on a serving plate.
- Frost with the following mixture:

1 8-ounce package cream cheese
1 clove garlic, minced
1/8 teaspoon Tabasco Sauce
1/4 cup mayonnaise

- Beat with an electric mixer then frost the Braunschweiger ball with mixture.
- Chill for 8 hours or overnight.
- Serve with crackers.

Anne Munger

Cross Village

Cross Village marks the northern most settlement of L'Arbre Croche. The popular belief is that Pere Marquette established the first mission in Cross Village. The probable origin of this belief is that the Native Americans say that "Kitchmekatewikwanaie," the Great Priest, established it.

Under the clapboarding is the old log church.

Prawn Paté

1½ ounces butter, softened
2 ounces cream cheese, softened
1 tablespoon mayonnaise
1/2 pound cooked prawns, chopped into small pieces
Tabasco Sauce to taste
A "good" pinch of nutmeg
1 small garlic clove, minced
2 teaspoons lemon juice

- Blend butter, cream cheese and mayonnaise together. Add all the other ingredients to mixture.
- Chill for several hours to blend flavors.
- This is good on buttered toast, French bread or as a stuffing in celery.

Patricia Clarke

A 1930s snowshoeing party sets out from the Clarke cottage porch.

"As Good as It Gets" Smoked Whitefish Paté

1 pound smoked whitefish, skinned and flaked
(available at Legs Inn in Cross Village)
12 ounces cream cheese, softened and cut into small
chunks
6 tablespoons unsalted butter, softened and cut into
bits
1 medium red onion, minced
1/4 cup fresh dill, chopped
1 tablespoon horseradish
2 tablespoons capers, drained
3 tablespoons fresh lemon juice
2 tablespoons cognac, optional or use additional lemon
juice
Freshly ground pepper

- Beat whitefish, cream cheese and butter in a mixing
  bowl with an electric mixer just until combined.
  Add onion, dill, horseradish, capers, lemon juice and
  cognac. Beat just until blended. Season to taste with
  pepper.

- Refrigerate at least 3 hours to blend flavors.

- Serve with water crackers.

Trina Hayes

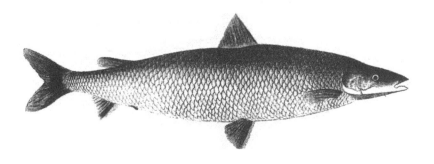

Chicken and Bacon Wrap

1¼ pound boneless, skinless chicken breast or chicken tenders
1 pound bacon
2/3 cup brown sugar, packed
2 tablespoons chili powder
1 lemon

- Preheat oven to 350⁰.
- Cut raw chicken into bite-size pieces.
- Cut the bacon slices into thirds.
- Wrap each chicken cube in a piece of bacon and insert a toothpick to hold together.
- Stir together brown sugar and chili powder in a small bowl.
- Dip bacon-wrapped chicken into brown sugar mixture.
- Line a broiler pan that has a wire rack with foil and spray with oil or non-stick spray.
- Place bacon-wrapped chicken on rack. Bake 30 – 40 minutes in the preheated 350⁰ oven until bacon is crispy.
- Place under broiler if additional crispiness is desired.
- Cut a lemon in half and place it on a dish for guests to insert used toothpicks in the lemon when done.

Alice Kelly

Chicken Log

2 8-ounce packages cream cheese, softened
1 teaspoon A-1 Sauce
1/2 teaspoon curry powder
1 garlic clove, finely minced
2 tablespoons onion, finely chopped
1½ cups cooked chicken, chopped (You may use canned.)
1/3 cup celery, minced
1/4 cup fresh parsley, chopped
1/4 cup almonds, chopped

- Mix the cream cheese, A-1 Sauce and curry powder together. Blend in garlic, onion, chicken and celery. Mix well.

- Add 2 tablespoons of parsley to the mixture.

- Divide mixture in half and roll into separate logs. Wrap each log in plastic wrap.

- Refrigerate at least 4 hours.

- When ready to serve, spread the remaining parsley and the chopped almonds on wax paper and roll the logs into the mixture.

- Serve with crackers or bagel chips.

- The chicken logs freeze well when tightly wrapped in plastic wrap.

Mary Rigby

What Really is a "Spring Chicken"?

Ida C. Bailey Allen, CBS's 1920s radio chef told listeners, "Chicken and fowl are always in season, even "spring" chickens being obtainable at other seasons thanks to the incubator. Turkeys are always best in the fall and early spring, ducks and geese from December to April and ducklings from early summer to fall. Theoretically, spring chicken is a bird under five months old, chicken anything from five months to a year, and fowl anything a year or older."

Ida C. Bailey Allen

Italian Sausage Nibbles

This is a long-time favorite with the Redpath Church coffee crowd who look for it whenever the Latimers welcome them to their cottage.

1/2 pound bulk sweet Italian sausage
1/2 pound bulk hot sausage
1 pound sharp cheddar cheese, grated
2¼ cups Bisquick baking mix*
1 tablespoon fennel seed
2 teaspoons oregano

- Preheat oven to 375⁰ if baking to serve without freezing.
- Mix sausages and cheese together then add biscuit mix and seasonings.
- Knead well.
- Shape into 1-inch balls.
- Bake for 15 minutes or until golden brown.
- Cool and freeze. Thaw and bake in a preheated 375⁰ oven for 3 minutes or until heated.

*Substitute 1 cup flour, 1½ teaspoons baking powder, 1/2 teaspoon salt, and 1 tablespoon oil or melted butter if you don't have Bisquick, a product General Mills sales executives adapted from a dining car chef they met in 1930.

Sara Latimer

Brie with Caramelized Cranberry Onion Chutney

We serve this on the Fourth of July when the entire family gathers in Good Hart. Use dried cherries or blueberries to fit the season.

2 tablespoons butter, melted in a 10" skillet
1 medium onion, thinly sliced and quartered
1/2 cup dried cranberries, blueberries or cherries,
  chopped
1 tablespoon packed brown sugar
1 tablespoon white balsamic vinegar
Cooking spray
1 round (15 ounces) Brie cheese
Unflavored water crackers

- Melt butter over medium heat. Cook onion in butter for 10 minutes, stirring frequently. Stir in berries, brown sugar and vinegar. Cook an additional 5 minutes, stirring frequently until mixture thickens and caramelizes.

- Preheat oven to 350⁰ and spray an ovenproof glass or pottery tart or pie pan with cooking spray. Place cheese on center of pan. Bake uncovered 10 – 15 minutes or until cheese is soft.

- Spoon cranberry and onion topping over cheese. Serve with unflavored water crackers.

- The topping can be made up to 24 hours ahead and covered and refrigerated. Reheat the topping in the microwave.

Trina Hayes

Cranberries in Michigan History

The "Ojibbeways" called them mashkigimin and considered them of great value. Cranberries grow in swamps ripening in October. All settlers joined in gathering and storing this bitter-sweet refreshing berry. The Native Americans preferred to pick them later in the winter. The fruit does not fall from the stem when ripe and will continue to ripen even beneath the snow. The juice was also used to dye porcupine quills red for decoration.

Good Hart resident Agnes Shenanaquet, 70, was chosen to attend, teach and exhibit at the 15th Annual Festival of Folk Art in 1981.

19

Cheese Ball with Seafood

1 8-ounce package cream cheese, softened
1 8-ounce package shredded cheddar cheese
1 small can minced clams, drained
1 small can tiny shrimp, drained
Lemon juice, a dash
Cocktail sauce

- Blend all ingredients well with an electric mixer. Form into a ball and refrigerate.
- Approximately 30 minutes before serving, remove ball from the refrigerator and cover with cocktail sauce.
- Serve with crackers.

Dixie Ira

Cheese Ball with Pimento

3 8-ounce packages cream cheese, softened
1 small jar pimento, drained
1 small bunch green onion, chopped fine
Ham, small dice

- Mix cream cheese with pimento and diced onion.
- Roll in chopped ham.
- Serve with crackers.

Dianna Hoffman

Baked Gouda

1 Gouda cheese round, wax covering removed
Dijon mustard
1 small package refrigerated crescent rolls

- Preheat oven to 375⁰.
- Slice cheese round in half horizontally, like two pancakes.
- Spread mustard in between the 2 cheese halves and on top of the cheese.
- Unroll crescent rolls and wrap around cheese.
- Bake until brown, following crescent roll directions.
- Serve with crackers.

Sally Kelsey

Bovee, Kelsey & Co.

Below the bluff in Cross Village, L. J. Bovee built a lumber mill in 1879. At one time this mill was reported to be the largest in Emmet County. Mr. L. A. Kelsey became a partner in 1881. Both men lived in Le Roy, N.Y. where they sought an on-site manager and partner, A. McVeen. Formerly a farmer, Mr. McVeen moved to Cross Village. The mill produced 2,500,000 feet of hardwood lumber a season which was shipped to Buffalo, engaging 50 to 60 teams drawing logs from the woods.

The Cross Village lumber mill

Cheese Chili Appetizers

10 eggs
1/2 cup butter or margarine, softened
1/2 cup flour
1 teaspoon baking powder
Salt to taste
2 4-ounce cans green chilies, chopped
1 pint cottage cheese
1 pound Monterey Jack cheese, grated

- Preheat oven to 400^0.
- Beat eggs lightly; add softened butter, flour, baking powder and salt and blend.
- Mix chilies, cottage cheese and Monterey Jack cheese and add to the first mixture.
- Turn into a greased 9" x 13" pan and bake for 15 minutes.
- Reduce heat to 350^0 and bake 30 minutes longer.
- Cut into squares and serve.
- This may be made ahead and reheated or frozen.

Mary Rigby

Stuffed Cheese Bread

SERVES 10

This is a favorite wherever I take it. It's definitely not healthy eating, but some things are worth the calories. People say, "I'll just have one more, then it's gone."

1 loaf frozen bread dough (such as Rich's)
2 cups Swiss cheese, shredded
2 cups cheddar cheese, shredded
1½ sticks butter
1/2 cup onion, chopped
2 teaspoons Spice Island Beau Monde seasoning
2 teaspoons dry mustard
1 teaspoon lemon juice
Poppy seeds

- Bake bread according to directions on package.
- Preheat oven to 350⁰.
- Slice bread diagonally at 1-inch intervals, top to bottom but DO NOT cut through lower crust.
- Turn the loaf a quarter turn to make a second diagonal cut (to create a crisscross effect).
- Stuff bread with Swiss cheese one direction, then cheddar the other.
- Melt butter. Mix with onion, seasonings and lemon juice. Pour butter mixture evenly over stuffed bread. Sprinkle with poppy seeds.
- Bake for 30 minutes.

Holly Hillier

A Jubilee of Bread

Originally from Prussia, Father John Weikamp arrived in Cross Village in 1855. At the time the Village was primarily Indian. He bought 350 acres and built a Catholic convent for over 200 brothers and nuns near the bluff above the lake. The mission was successful under his strict tenure, raising a chapel, dormitories, school, barn, gristmill, steam saw mill, carpenter and blacksmith shops.

To celebrate his fiftieth year of religious service and knowing that his Indian parishioners could not afford a celebration, Weikamp requested that his nuns cook 1,000 pounds of bread that he distributed. They gave 25 pounds of bread to each Native American family his mission served.

Rev. Joannes Bern. Weikamp.

23

Virginia Thomas's Party Pumpernickel

Carolyn Sutherland, current owner of the Good Hart Store, says her own recipes "never have more than three ingredients made in one pan." She loves "memory" recipes from Good Hart neighbors who are no longer here. Virginia Thomas, "Mom Tom," was one of the grand ladies of Lamkin Road who shared both her smiles and her recipes.

1/2 cup green onions, chopped including greens
6 strips bacon, cooked, drained and crumbled
3/4 cup sharp cheddar cheese, grated
3/4 cup Miracle Whip
Worcestershire Sauce, a dash
Party Pumpernickel bread

- Mix all ingredients.
- Spread on Party Pumpernickel bread slices.
- Broil 2 – 3 minutes until the cheese melts.

Virginia Thomas
via Carolyn Sutherland

Glazed Red Pepper-Fennel Almonds

MAKES 1 CUP

I serve these for special openings at Three Pines Studio in Cross Village.

3 tablespoons sugar
2 teaspoons fennel seeds
1 teaspoon dried crushed red pepper
1 teaspoon salt
1 cup whole almonds
1 tablespoon water

- Preheat oven to 325^0.
- Line a heavy baking sheet with foil; spray with nonstick spray.
- Combine sugar, fennel seeds, crushed red pepper and salt in a medium bowl. Mix in almonds and 1 tablespoon water.
- Spread mixture on prepared baking sheet in a single layer.
- Bake until sugar melts and almonds are deep golden brown and glazed, stirring often, for approximately 22 minutes.
- Separate almonds with a fork; cool completely on the baking sheet.
- These keep for a week in a plastic bag or sealed container and last much longer if refrigerated.

Joann Condino

Storage

The Native Americans solved part of the problem of storing preserved food by making makaks or birch bark boxes. Birch bark has an amazing ability to withstand rot and when tallowed on its inner surface is nearly airtight.

Wigwassi makak

Nutty Cracker Delights

1 sleeve (44) club crackers
1 stick butter
1/2 cup sugar
1 teaspoon vanilla
Almonds or pecans

- Preheat oven to 350^0.
- Line a cookie pan (jelly roll type) with the club crackers.
- Melt the butter and sugar in a sauce pan and boil 2 minutes.
- Remove from heat and add vanilla.
- Pour over crackers and sprinkle with almonds or pecans.
- Bake for 8 – 10 minutes or until lightly browned.
- Remove from pan <u>immediately</u> and transfer to wire racks.
- Store in an airtight container.

Mary Rigby

Jezebel Sauce

Keep on hand and treat unexpected guests to this easy appetizer.

36 ounces apple jelly
36 ounces apricot-pineapple preserves (or substitute
 apricot, pineapple or peach)
5 ounces horseradish
2 ounces dry mustard
2 tablespoons coarse black or white pepper

- Mix all ingredients together with a whisk or an electric mixer and ladle into jars.

- Refrigerate.

- Serve over cream cheese with crackers or as a spicy sauce with meats.

- Store-brand jellies and preserves come in 12 ounce jars: buy 3 of each, wash them and refill with Jezebel Sauce. Add a label and bow on the lid and you have a nice gift. This makes 7 jars so you'll need an extra jar.

Anne Munger

1901: How to Drive Away Mosquitoes

When mosquitoes are about, these pests can dampen the mood of any outdoor festivity. Burn a piece of camphor, the size of a walnut, on a plate. Place camphor pieces around the cabin, off season, in those nooks where mice have been seen. They, too, dislike the odor.

Oyster Cracker Nibblers

Our family loves this at Thanksgiving and Christmas. We give it as gifts in small decorative tins to members of the family.

1 20-ounce bag oyster crackers
1 cup vegetable oil
1/2 teaspoon garlic powder
3 teaspoons dill weed
3 teaspoons lemon pepper
1/2 ounce dry ranch dressing mix

- Stir oil, garlic powder, dill weed, lemon pepper and ranch dressing mix together in a large bowl.

- Add crackers and stir every 15 minutes for an hour until absorbed.

- Store in a tin container or in a tightly closed plastic bag.

Debbie Dicken

Bread, Breakfast & Brunch

The beach at Good Hart/Middle Village, 1950s, by Cliff Powers

Recipes

French Bread "Le Vrai"

3 cups bread flour
1/4+ teaspoon granular yeast
1¼ teaspoons salt
1⅝ cups water

- Start this bread at least 21 hours before you want to eat it. Combine flour, yeast and salt in a mixing bowl. Add 1 and 5/8 cups water and stir until blended. Dough will be shaggy and sticky. Cover bowl with plastic wrap and let rise at least 12 hours, preferably 18 hours. Dough is ready when the surface is dotted with bubbles.

- Turn the dough out onto a lightly floured work surface. Sprinkle with a little more flour and fold it over itself once or twice. Cover with plastic wrap and let rest for 15 minutes. Meanwhile spread out a 1 foot square piece of parchment paper on a tea towel (not terry). Sprinkle parchment paper with flour. Using just enough flour to keep the dough from sticking to your fingers, quickly shape the dough into a ball and place it seam side down on the floured parchment paper. Cover with a second well-floured cotton towel and let it rise until doubled, about 2 hours.

- Set a cast iron or other heavy 6 to 8 quart covered pot or Dutch oven in the oven. The pot and lid must be able to withstand a 450⁰ oven. Preheat oven to 450⁰ about 30 minutes before the end of the second rise. When the dough is ready, carefully remove the pot from the oven, slide your hand under the towel and turn the dough over into the pot, seam side up. Shake the pot if needed but the dough doesn't have to be perfect. Cover the pot and bake for 30 minutes. Remove the lid and bake an additional 15 minutes until the top is beautifully browned. Remove from pot and cool on a rack.

Trina Hayes

Grist Mill

There was a "close enough" grist mill down on Five Mile Creek for our local pioneers. Grist is grain that is to be ground or has been ground.

Elliott's Mill at Five Mile Creek was used for dances and roller skating.

A Heritage Recipe . . .

Hemlock House Kalachi or Rich Rolls

These are the basis for the memorable Hemlock House cinnamon rolls and hamburger buns.

1 package yeast for each 2 cups liquid
1 tablespoon sugar
1/4 cup water
1¾ cups milk at room temperature
1 teaspoon salt
Flour
2 tablespoons butter or margarine, melted
1 egg, beaten

- Add sugar to yeast and mix with 1/4 cup warm water until dissolved.

- Stir in milk, salt and enough sifted flour for sponge (a soft batter).

- Add melted butter or margarine and the beaten egg.

- Add more flour for soft dough. Knead and let double. Punch down and let rise again.

- Form into rolls. Let rise again.

- Preheat oven to 375⁰ – 400⁰ and bake for 9 minutes. Turn in oven and bake 9 more minutes.

Ruby Wyland – Heritage Recipe

The wannigan is the raft with the cook house on it.

Batter Bread

Adina Foster (Mrs. Ralph Foster) gave me this recipe many years ago.

2½ cups warm water
2 packages yeast
4 tablespoons shortening
4 tablespoons sugar
4 teaspoons salt
6 cups flour

- Dissolve yeast in water. Blend in shortening, sugar and salt.

- Add 2 cups flour. Beat well with a spoon or electric mixer. Add the rest of the flour and mix until the dough leaves the sides of the bowl and the flour is blended.

- Cover and allow to rise out of drafts until double in bulk. Beat down.

- Divide in half. Spread in greased loaf pans. Let rise to the top of the pans.

- Preheat oven to 375⁰ and bake about 30 to 40 minutes.

- Remove and let cool.

Georgie Richner

The first Richner cottage was a Good Hart home-steader which was moved from a farm to the shore. There was no running water or electricity.

Melt-in-Your-Mouth Dinner Rolls

2 tablespoons dry yeast
2 cups warm water, divided
1 cup vegetable oil
1 cup white sugar
3 eggs
6-8 cups flour

- Mix yeast and 1 cup of warm water. Let mixture proof until it bubbles.
- Mix oil, sugar and 1 cup of warm water. Add 3 eggs and beat well.
- Add oil mixture into the yeast mixture. Stir in flour 2 cups at a time until no longer sticky.
- Cover with a towel and let rise until double in size.
- Preheat oven to 350⁰.
- Grease a 10" x 15" pan or two 9" x 13" pans.
- Shape dough into rolls in pans and let rise again.
- Bake for 30 minutes. Butter tops of baked rolls and let cool on a wire rack.
- The recipe can also be shaped into 2 to 3 bread pans for delicious bread.

Jaci Krieg

Cross Village after 1889, when the Franciscans completed the church and built the rectory and school

Beer Bread

3 cups self-rising flour
3 tablespoons sugar
1 can beer

- Preheat oven to 375⁰.
- Mix ingredients together with a wooden spoon.
- Spoon into a large loaf pan — three quarters full.
- Bake for 40 minutes.

Betty Graham from Carolyn Sutherland

The Graham ladies host a beach social at Chippewa Cove in 1917.

Native American Corn — Hearing History

A story told by Frank Et-tawageshik, a former tribal chairman of the Little Traverse Bay Bands of Odawa Indians, illustrates how history can be remembered in the smallest ways. When Frank spoke with an elderly white man (chemokemon) about his childhood recollections of a festival in Charlevoix, the man mentioned that his family had parked their car by the lake. Native Americans also drove their Model T's to the beach area where they camped on a large spit of sand. The old man recalled being in his car where he'd been tucked in by his parents and had heard a wop-wop-wop sound. Frank explained to the man that what he heard was the sound of history; the Odawa were making bread. Fires that heated the sand were scraped aside and bread dough was placed on the sand then covered with more heated sand. When the bread was done, it was dug up and tossed back and forth between two paddles to remove the sand, causing the "wop-wop-wop" sound as the bread hit the paddles.

Johnny Cake

(Journey Cake or Ash Cake)

Adapted from a Native American original recipe

6 slices bacon, chopped
2 tablespoons bacon fat
1 cup yellow corn meal
1 cup flour
1/3 cup sugar
2 teaspoons baking powder
1 teaspoon salt
1 large egg
1 cup milk

- Preheat oven to 425°.
- Fry the chopped bacon and drain well on paper towels. Grease the bottom and sides of a shallow 8" x 8" baking dish with bacon fat. Reserve 2 tablespoons of bacon fat for batter.
- Whisk corn meal, flour, sugar, baking powder and salt together in a mixing bowl.
- Set the baking dish in the preheated oven.
- Beat the egg in a small mixing bowl. Whisk in the milk and reserved bacon fat. Add the bacon and stir into the dry ingredient mixture just until well blended.
- Pour into the hot baking dish and bake 20 minutes. Serve immediately.

A Heritage Recipe . . .

May's Orange Biscuits

2 cups flour
4 teaspoons baking powder
1 teaspoon salt
1/4 teaspoon cream of tartar
1/2 cup Crisco or Spry shortening
2/3 cup milk
Softened butter
Rind of 2 oranges, grated
2 tablespoons granulated sugar

- Preheat oven to 400⁰.
- Sift flour, baking powder, salt and cream of tartar twice. Cut in the shortening. Add milk and roll out quite thin.
- Mix grated orange rind with sugar.
- Spread dough with softened butter. Sprinkle with half of the sugar and orange rind mixture. Roll up like a jelly roll and slice into 3/4" slices.
- Dip top side of each slice in the remaining sugar and orange rind mixture.
- Grease the baking sheet and bake about 7 to 10 minutes.

Bonnie Bliss Weitzel

The Wigwam Restaurant

Blisswood

This is a recipe from the collection of May C. Bliss. She and her husband Chauncey owned Blisswood, and from the 1940s until 1982 had cottages for summer rental. May and her mother-in-law were owners of the Wigwam, a restaurant on the Bliss property, where they served meals by reservation in the 1920–1940 era. Then Chauncey and May built the Krude Kraft Lodge in 1936, and began serving meals there. May later served only breakfasts to guests in the cottages and lodge continuing this until she was 80 years old. Chicken and dumplings and planked whitefish were guests' favorites as were these orange biscuits.

Blueberry Muffins

Our family enjoys these with corn chowder every summer.

2½ cups flour
4 teaspoons baking powder
1/2 teaspoon salt
1/2 cup sugar
1/4 cup butter
1 egg
1 cup milk
1 teaspoon vanilla
1½ cups blueberries

TOPPING:
1/2 cup sugar
1/2 teaspoon cinnamon
1/3 cup flour
1/4 cup butter

- Preheat oven to 375⁰.
- Sift flour, baking powder and salt. Cream together sugar, butter and egg. Add the dry ingredients to the butter mixture.
- Mix together milk and vanilla and add all at once to batter, stirring until blended. Fold in blueberries.
- Spoon into 12 greased muffin cups.
- Combine the sugar, cinnamon and flour for the topping and cut in 1/4 cup butter to make crumbles. Sprinkle topping over muffins. Bake for 20 to 25 minutes.

Susan Carson

Bran Muffins

These were a big hit when we owned the "Out to Lunch" restaurant in Harbor Springs.

2 cups Bran Buds
1 cup boiling water
1½ cups sugar
1/2 cup shortening
2 eggs
1/2 teaspoon salt
2½ cups flour
2½ teaspoons baking soda
1 cup All Bran
2 tablespoons baking powder
2 cups buttermilk

- Preheat oven to 425^0.
- Soak Bran Buds in boiling water for 30 minutes.
- Mix sugar, shortening, eggs, salt, flour, baking soda, All Bran, baking powder and buttermilk. Blend well. Add soaked Bran Buds. Mix well.
- Grease and flour a large 12-cup muffin tin. Pour into muffin tin.
- Bake for 40 to 45 minutes.

Dixie Ira

In earlier Michigan days it was thought that carrying a "buckeye" or horse chestnut in your pocket warded off rheumatism.

Six-Week Bran Muffins

I make a batch of this in the summer and use as needed for guests.

4 beaten eggs
3 cups sugar or Splenda
1 cup oil
5 cups flour
2 teaspoons salt
5 teaspoons baking soda
1 teaspoon cinnamon
1 quart (4 cups) buttermilk
1 20-ounce package Raisin Bran cereal
1 cup raisins

- Preheat oven to 400^0.
- Mix sugar and oil in a large mixing bowl. Add beaten eggs, then the rest of the ingredients. Mix well. Pour desired amount into muffin tins. Store remainder in a covered bowl in the refrigerator and use as needed.
- Bake for 15 to 20 minutes.

Marge Edwards

Banana Muffins

3/4 cup sugar
1/4 cup butter, softened
1 egg, beaten
3 large, ripe bananas, mashed
1½ cups flour
1 teaspoon baking soda
1 tablespoon baking powder

- Preheat oven to 350^0.
- Cream sugar and butter together well. Add egg and mashed bananas.
- Add all dry ingredients and mix well. Pour into a greased muffin tin.
- Bake for 30 minutes checking the tops so they don't burn.

Marti Wallen

Easy Pumpkin Muffins

1 box spice cake mix
1 small can pumpkin
2 eggs
1/4 cup water

- Preheat oven to 350^0.
- Mix all ingredients together until smooth; don't over mix.
- Grease or line muffin tins and fill with batter.
- Bake for 12 to 15 minutes or until a toothpick inserted comes out clean.

Laura Ward

Chief Ignatius Petoskey and his family held reserved land at Seven Mile Point.

Primitive Images Good Hart and Soul Tea Room

The tea room is located in the center of Downtown Good Hart. The historic 1850s square-hewn log building was moved to Good Hart in 1997 by owner Ceci Bauer. Rustic furnishings and the tea room offer a great place to retreat and relax with a warm cup of tea.

Masala Chai tea is one of the tea room's most popular teas and is made from the spices cardamom, nutmeg, cinnamon, pepper, and of course, Darjeeling black tea.

"Good Harted" Chai Muffins

1/2 cup canola oil
1 cup white sugar
2 eggs, slightly beaten
3 medium bananas (very ripe)
2 cups whole wheat flour
1/2 teaspoon salt
1 teaspoon baking soda
1/2 cup toasted wheat germ
1/2 cup Masala Chai tea,* brewed strong!
3/4 cup walnuts, pecans or macadamia nuts (slightly chopped)

GLAZE:
1/4 cup Masala Chai tea,* brewed strong!
1 cup confectioners' sugar
*To make Masala Chai tea, use 2 teaspoons Masala Chai tea to 1 cup water and steep for 5 minutes.

- Preheat oven to 350°.
- Blend oil, sugar, beaten eggs and mashed bananas in a mixing bowl and set aside.
- Combine whole wheat flour, salt and baking soda and slowly add to banana mixture. Slowly add wheat germ, 1/2 cup of tea and slightly chopped nuts and blend.
- Fill 12-cup muffin tin. Bake for 25 to 30 minutes.
- When cool, drizzle with glaze of 1/4 cup strongly brewed Masala Chai tea* mixed with 1 cup confectioners' sugar.

Ceci Bauer

Date Nut Bread

1 pound chopped dates
2 cups boiling water
2 teaspoons baking soda
2 tablespoons shortening or butter
2 cups white sugar
3 eggs
2 teaspoons vanilla
4 cups sifted flour
1/2 teaspoon salt
1 cup chopped nuts

- Preheat oven to 350^0.
- Pour boiling water over dates. Add baking soda and let cool.
- Cream shortening or butter with sugar and eggs.
- Stir the cooled dates into the creamed mixture.
- Stir in vanilla, flour, salt and nuts.
- Pour into a greased loaf pan.
- Bake for 40 to 60 minutes.

Marti Wallen

What was a Mossback?

After the Native Americans had chosen the land they reserved, the upper part of Lower Michigan was opened for homesteading. Folks flocked to Traverse City to register for a "forty." This land was given free of charge if the registrant would "prove it up" (build a dwelling, clear the land for crops and plant it). Many came with little more than the clothes they wore. What they had they carried to their land. They placed cushions of moss between them and the loads they carried on their backs: mossbacks!

Pistachio Nut Bread

My aunt Clarice made this for all our family gatherings.

1 box yellow cake mix
1 package instant pistachio pudding
4 eggs
1/2 pint (1 cup) sour cream
1/4 cup salad oil
1/4 cup water

SUGAR MIXTURE:
1 teaspoon cinnamon
1 cup ground nuts
3/4 cup sugar

- Preheat oven to 350⁰.
- Mix cake mix, pudding, eggs, sour cream, salad oil and water together.
- Pour two-thirds of the batter into 2 well-greased loaf pans or 3 small ones.
- Sprinkle with half of sugar mixture. Spoon remaining batter on top and sprinkle with remaining sugar mixture.
- Bake for 40 to 45 minutes if using two pans. Bake for less time if using 3 pans.

Pat Burns

Bishop's Bread

1 cup whole maraschino cherries, drained
1 cup sweet or milk chocolate chunks
1 cup Brazil nuts cut in half
1 cup walnuts, do not chop
1 cup dates, cut in half, or substitute dried apricots
3/4 cup sugar
3/4 cup flour
1/2 teaspoon baking powder
1/2 teaspoon salt
3 eggs
1 tablespoon brandy

- Preheat oven to 325⁰.
- Mix cherries, chocolate, nuts and dates in a large bowl.
- Sift sugar, flour, baking powder and salt over the fruit and nut mixture.
- Beat eggs lightly; add brandy to eggs and pour over fruit and nut mixture and mix well.
- Line a greased 9" x 5" x 3" loaf pan with wax paper. Grease the wax paper. Turn the mixture into the pan and press firmly.
- Bake for 1 hour and 35 minutes or longer if baking several loaves.
- Cool on a rack for 10 minutes. Remove wax paper while warm. Cool completely. Wrap in a brandy soaked cheese cloth, plastic wrap and aluminum foil. Place in a plastic bag and refrigerate.

Harriet Jackson

Bishop Frederic Baraga, the first Bishop of Marquette, served the Native American churches of L'Arbre Croche in the mid-1800s.

The Lamkin family are long-time residents dating back to 1880s. Lowell Lamkin founded his general store which became the memorable Lamkin Lakeshore Lodge in the 1930s. It was located on Lamkin Road below Good Hart.

An Indian Art Store, once situated on the bluff above the Lamkin Lodge on Lake Shore Drive, sold Native American crafts to resort era tourists.

Cinnamon Rolls

1 cup milk, 75⁰ – 85⁰ F
1 large egg
4 tablespoons butter or margarine
3 tablespoons sugar
1/2 teaspoon salt
3⅓ cups flour
2 teaspoons active dry yeast OR
1½ teaspoons bread machine/fast rise yeast

CINNAMON FILLING:
1/4 cup butter
3/4 cup brown or white sugar
Cinnamon
1/2 cup raisins or nuts, optional

SUGAR GLAZE:
1 cup confectioners' sugar
1/2 tablespoon milk
1/2 teaspoon vanilla
1 tablespoon butter, melted

With a bread machine:

- Add the first 8 ingredients in the order listed to the bread maker pan. Program the bread machine for dough.

- When finished, turn the dough out of the bread pan and punch down, then let rest for 15 minutes.

- Preheat oven to 375^0.

- Roll out a rectangle, about 15 x 10 inches (dough may be divided into 2 pieces to make rolling easier). Spread with 2 tablespoons of butter within an inch along the long edge. Sprinkle with sugar and cinnamon. If desired, add raisins and/or nuts. Roll dough tightly on the long side making it 15 inches long. Press dough edge together to seal the edge. With a sharp knife, cut into 1 inch slices and place in 2 greased 9" x 13" baking pans.

- Let rise to double size, about 30 to 40 minutes. Bake in a preheated 375^0 oven for 20 to 25 minutes or until golden brown. Do not over bake! When done, loosen from the pan and cool. If desired, add sugar glaze to top of rolls.

Without a bread machine:

- Add butter to the warm milk then add egg, sugar, salt and yeast. Mix, then add flour and knead for 10 minutes. Let rise in $75^0 - 85^0$ area until doubled in volume. Punch down and let rest for 15 minutes. Follow remainder of recipe above.

- To make the sugar glaze, mix all glaze ingredients together. Spread on rolls and let set to harden the glaze.

Janet Lamkin

Variation: substitute 2/3 cup maple syrup for the sugar and leave out the cranberries, cherries, orange rind and orange juice.

Jo's Scones

These are great to have on hand for breakfast or with a cup of tea when folks stop by.

1/2 cup sugar
1 cup quick oats
2½ cups flour
1½ tablespoons baking powder
1/2 teaspoon salt
2 eggs
3/4 cup milk
1 stick butter, melted
1 cup dried cherries or cranberries
1 tablespoon grated orange rind
2 tablespoons frozen orange juice concentrate
3/4 cup chopped walnuts

- Cut two 10" circles of parchment paper. Use 1 to line a 10-inch round cake pan such as a springform pan. Reserve the second piece.
- Mix sugar, quick oats, flour, baking powder and salt together. Add eggs, milk and melted butter and mix together. Add dried cherries or cranberries, orange rind, orange juice concentrate and walnuts and mix together.
- Place the dough in the lined cake pan and press into an even layer. Cover the dough with the second parchment paper. Cover with foil. Freeze until the dough is very firm (at least 12 hours). Note: after about 2 hours take the dough out and cut it into 12 pieces while it is firm, but not yet frozen.
- Preheat the oven to 350⁰ and thaw the dough for 5 minutes at room temperature. Turn out of the cake pan. Break off the pieces you wish to cook and return the rest to the freezer. Place scone pieces on a greased baking sheet. Brush with milk or frozen orange juice concentrate. Sprinkle with coarse sugar.
- Bake until golden brown approximately 20 to 25 minutes.

Jo Cunningham

Scottish Potato Scones

My mother made this dish as a treat on Sunday mornings. She had a round griddle, which she set on top of the stove and cooked on gas burners set low. It was always a success because this recipe used basic ingredients which were ready at hand, could be cooked quickly, and fed many. (There were five of us children, plus father and mother.)

My father put marmalade on his scones. When I was very young, I thought that my adored mother was the only one who could cook potato scones because she was born in Scotland.

1/2 pound boiled and mashed potatoes
3 tablespoons butter, melted
1/2 teaspoon salt
1/2 cup plus 1 tablespoon (2.5 ounces) flour

- Mash the potatoes while they are still warm and add the butter and salt.

- Add in enough flour to make the dough pliable without making it too dry. The type of potato will determine this.

- Turn out onto a floured surface and roll until about 1/4" thick. Cut into 6-inch diameter circles and then into quarters.

- Prick all over with a fork and cook in a heavy pan or griddle which has been lightly greased.

- Cook each side for 3 minutes or until golden brown. (To add more calories, put cheese between two scones; cook until cheese is melted.)

Mary Groves

Oven Omelet

This can be made ahead and refrigerated before baking.

1 pound bacon, cut into small pieces
4 green onions, chopped
10 eggs
2 cups milk
1/2 teaspoon salt
1/8 teaspoon nutmeg
2½ cups Swiss cheese (10 ounces), shredded
1/2 pound boiled ham, cut in strips

- Preheat oven to 350^0.
- Brown and drain the bacon saving 2 tablespoons of bacon grease. Sauté the green onions in the bacon grease.
- Beat eggs and stir in remaining ingredients except for a handful each of bacon and cheese for topping.
- Pour mixture into a greased 9" x 13" baking dish. Bake for 35 to 40 minutes. Sprinkle with remaining cheese and bacon and let stand for 10 minutes before serving.

The spring below the bluff at Good Hart was an essential stop when your cottage didn't have running water.

Christmas Omelet

This can be made the day before and refrigerated which is nice for a busy Christmas morning. It is our family favorite.

2 pounds hot sausage (bulk), browned and drained
 (or use 1 pound hot and 1 pound sweet)
12 ounces sharp cheddar cheese, shredded
1 8-ounce package of refrigerator crescent rolls
2 cups frozen hash brown potatoes (loose pack)
1 onion, chopped
1 green pepper, chopped
Mushrooms, sautéed, optional
9 eggs, beaten
1/2 cup milk
Salt and pepper to taste
Parmesan cheese, grated
Oregano, to taste

- Preheat oven to 375^0.
- Press rolls in the bottom of a 9" x 13" baking dish. Seal perforations.
- Spoon sausage over dough. Add hash brown potatoes, onion, green pepper, mushrooms and shredded cheese.
- Combine eggs, milk, salt and pepper and pour over all.
- Bake approximately 50 minutes.
- Sprinkle with Parmesan cheese and oregano. Return to oven to bake an additional 5 minutes.

Sally Kelsey

Lumber Camp Hash Browns

In the late 1800s, a local lumber camp cook remarked, "there's more to warming up 'taters than most women know." (These 'taters were either leftovers from evening chow or they were cooked prior to breakfast.) "You have to get the meat fryings just so hot – almost smoking – before the 'taters are put in the iron skillet. Then you chop them with a tin can until they're pretty fine. Brown them and turn them two or three times and they are fine, not at all like the soggy ones you get in a restaurant."

Redpath Memorial Church

The "Little Stone Church" (Redpath Memorial Presbyterian) was built in Cross Village after the 1918 fire. Currently area residents hold Sunday services from Memorial Day to Labor Day. Famous resort architect Earl Mead designed the church and his grand "cottages" of the Victorian era are still points of pride at Harbor Point, Bay View and Wequetonsing.

Presbyterian Eggs

6 hard-boiled eggs, peeled and sliced
1 cup mayonnaise (light mayonnaise may be used)
2/3 cup milk
1 can cream of mushroom soup
6 slices bacon, cooked and drained
8 ounces mushrooms, sliced and sautéed (optional)

- Preheat oven to 350^0.
- Mix mayonnaise, milk and soup in a casserole dish.
- Add the eggs and mushrooms and stir.
- Bake for 30 minutes.
- Serve over toasted English muffins and top with a slice of bacon.
- The bacon may also be crumbled and stirred into the eggs.

Betty Little
via Linda Little

The First Presbyterian Church of Cross Village (1890-1918) before the Village fire

Breakfast Pizza

This miracle recipe is good for breakfast, lunch, dinner, brunch or as an appetizer. I recently doubled the recipe and spread it on a cookie sheet, baked it, and cut it into small squares for the Redpath Church coffee.

1 8-ounce package of refrigerator crescent rolls
6 eggs, beaten
1/2 pound bacon, cooked, drained and crumbled
1½ cups cheddar cheese, shredded
1 4-ounce can sliced mushrooms
Optional additions: tomatoes, olives, peppers, onion, spinach, asparagus

- Preheat oven to 375^0.
- Unroll dough and press into a 12-inch pizza pan. This will take a while; press till very thin.
- Combine eggs, bacon, cheese, mushrooms and other chosen ingredients. Pour over dough.
- Bake for 15 to 20 minutes.

Janie Richter

Church Coffee "Sharing" Recipes

After each Redpath Church Service we gather at members' homes for coffee and fellowship. The church coffees always bring out the most wonderful "sharing" recipes and this is one of them.

Jane Richter's family, the Piltz family, came with the Apple family to Cross Village in the mid-1960s when the Redpath Church reopened. Our parents enjoyed many years of retirement here and we are all continuing the tradition.

The Redpath Church, designed by Earl Mead, replaced the First Presbyterian Church.

Sausage Mushroom Casserole

This and other casserole recipes became standards when we traveled north for the weekend with friends. It was easy to make ahead — then we had time to enjoy our company while we were in our favorite place. Now that we live in Good Hart, this recipe has become a standard when friends and family visit.

1 pound bulk sausage, browned and drained
10 eggs, lightly beaten
3 cups milk
2 teaspoons dry mustard
6 cups cubed bread
2 cups sharp cheddar cheese, shredded
1/2 teaspoon black pepper
1/2 cup mushrooms, sliced (optional)
1 medium tomato, seeded and chopped (optional)
1/2 cup green onion, sliced (optional)

- Preheat oven to 325⁰.
- In a large bowl, combine eggs, milk and mustard.
- Distribute half of the bread in a buttered 9" x 13" baking dish.
- Sprinkle with half the pepper and half the cheese. Top with half the sausage and other optional ingredients. Repeat layering.
- Pour egg mixture over casserole.
- Bake in a preheated 325⁰ oven for 60 minutes.

Bonnie Weitzel

The beach at Good Hart as seen in the 1940s, Photo by Cliff Powers

Roxie's Green Chili Pie

This was my husband's grandmother's recipe. It's been a family favorite for Sunday brunches or as an appetizer on football weekends. It can be doubled or tripled and baked in a larger casserole dish for larger crowds.

1 can green chilies, seeded
2 cups grated cheeses (1⅓ cup Monterey Jack and 2/3 cup longhorn cheese) (You may substitute other cheeses.)
4 eggs, beaten
Salsa, optional

- Preheat oven to 375^0.
- Spread chilies on the bottom of a pie plate or quiche dish. Cover with grated cheeses. Pour beaten eggs on top.
- Bake for 45 minutes.
- Serve with salsa if desired as this is a southwest-type brunch dish.

Pat Dobson

Breakfast Casserole

This recipe may cut in half and made in one casserole dish.

1 large loaf of Italian or French bread, broken into small pieces
6 tablespoons butter, melted
3/4 pound Swiss cheese, grated
1/2 pound Monterey Jack cheese, grated
9 slices salami, chopped
16 eggs
3¼ cups milk
1/4 cup dry white wine
4 green onions, chopped
1 tablespoon Dijon mustard
1/2 teaspoon salt
1/4 teaspoon pepper
1½ cups sour cream
2/3 cup Parmesan cheese, grated

- Butter two 9" x 13" pans.
- Divide bread pieces, place in pans and drizzle with melted butter.
- Sprinkle with Swiss cheese, Monterey Jack cheese and salami.
- Beat together eggs, milk, wine, green onions, mustard, salt and pepper and pour into pans.
- Cover and refrigerate overnight.
- Preheat the oven to 325°. Cover the casseroles with foil and bake for 1 hour.
- Remove the foil and top with sour cream and sprinkle with Parmesan cheese.
- Bake an additional 10 – 15 minutes.

Mary Rigby

Spinach and Cheese Frittata

This reheats very well so it can be made ahead and reheated.

1/2 cup butter
3 eggs
1 cup flour
1 cup whole milk
1 teaspoon salt
1 teaspoon baking powder
1 pound (4 cups) cheese, grated (I use 1/2 Gruyere and 1/2 Swiss but you can also use Jack cheese.)
4 cups fresh spinach

- Preheat oven to 350^0.
- Melt butter in a 7" x 11" baking dish.
- Beat eggs and add remaining ingredients. Blend well.
- Pour spinach mixture over melted butter.
- Bake 40 – 45 minutes until golden brown. Cool 10 minutes.

Pat Dobson

Janet McFarland, center, hosts a Good Hart beach breakfast, July, 1927.

Sausage Apple Ring

For a special presentation, fill the center of the ring with scrambled eggs.

2 pounds bulk sausage
30 saltine crackers, crushed (about 1½ cups)
2 eggs, slightly beaten
1/2 cup milk
1/4 cup onion, finely chopped
1 cup apple, finely chopped

- Preheat oven to 350⁰.
- Combine all ingredients and press lightly into a greased 6-cup ring mold.
- Turn out onto a shallow roasting pan.
- Bake for 1 hour. Drain and turn out onto a serving dish.

Laurelynne Harris

Brown Sugar Bacon

This is also delicious as an hors d'oeuvre — try not to eat it before you serve it.

**Brown sugar
Bacon**

- With your fingers, work brown sugar into each bacon strip, on both sides.
- To cook the bacon on the stovetop, slowly fry the bacon in a skillet at a low temperature until it is fully cooked, but not crisp (the sugar will make it crisp).
- You may also bake it in a regular oven or toaster oven on a flat pan (with or without foil) in a preheated 350^0 oven for approximately 10 minutes.
- The sugar tends to cook more quickly than the bacon so watch it carefully.
- Remove from the oven when the bacon is cooked but not crisp.
- Place cooked bacon slices on wax paper; it will crisp up.

Holly Hillier

Tom and Eliza King sugaring at Middle Village

57

SHORE DRIVE SCENE
CROSS VILLAGE, MICH

Salmon Quiche

This salmon quiche recipe was my mother's and was her favorite for luncheons with friends or for bridal showers. It also makes a great light summer meal served with fruit or on a green salad.

CRUST:
1 cup whole wheat or white flour
2/3 cup sharp cheddar cheese, shredded
1/4 cup almonds, chopped
1/2 teaspoon salt
1/4 teaspoon paprika
6 tablespoons oil

FILLING:
1 (15 ounce) can salmon, drained. (Reserve liquid and add water to make 1/2 cup.)
3 eggs, beaten
1 cup sour cream
1/4 cup mayonnaise
1/2 cup sharp cheddar cheese, grated
1 tablespoon onion, grated
1/4 teaspoon dried dill weed
3 drops bottled hot pepper sauce

- Preheat oven to 400^0.
- Prepare crust by combining flour, cheese, almonds, salt and paprika in a bowl. Stir in the oil. Set aside 1/2 cup of the crust mixture.
- Press remaining mixture into the bottom and up the sides of a 9-inch quiche dish or pie plate. Bake the crust for 10 minutes. Remove crust from oven.
- Reduce oven temperature to 325^0.
- Flake the salmon, removing the bones and skin; set aside.
- In a bowl, blend together the eggs, sour cream, mayonnaise and reserved salmon and water liquid. Stir in the salmon, cheese, onion, dill weed and hot pepper sauce.
- Spoon filling into crust. Sprinkle with reserved crust mixture.
- Bake in 325^{0}oven for 45 minutes or until firm in center and a knife comes out clean.
- Serve warm or at room temperature.

Pat Dobson

A Commercial Fishing Team from Cross Village

The lumber mill is in the middle ground.

Both fishing and lumbering were main sources of year-round income in the area. When the lumber was gone and the 1918 fire was followed by a deadly flu and the railroad took another route to Mackinaw City, there was little incentive to rebuild Cross Village.

Joni Dickens' Favorite Quiche

1¼ cups baking mix such as Bisquick* or Jiffy brand
1/4 cup butter or margarine, softened
2 tablespoons boiling water
1 cup sharp cheddar cheese, shredded
4 turkey sausage links, cooked and sliced
1/4 cup green pepper, diced
1/4 cup tomato, diced
1½ cups half and half
3 eggs or egg substitute equivalent
Onion powder, garlic powder and pepper to taste
*Substitute 1 cup flour, 1½ teaspoons baking powder,
  1/2 teaspoon salt, and 1 tablespoon oil or melted
  butter for the Bisquick baking mix.

- Preheat oven to 400⁰.
- Grease a 9" x 1¼" pie plate or comparable glass baking dish.
- Stir baking mix and butter until blended. Add boiling water and stir vigorously until soft dough forms.
- Press dough on the bottom and up the sides of the baking dish, forming the crust.
- Sprinkle cheese, sausage, green pepper and tomato over the crust.
- Beat half and half and eggs together; stir in spices. Pour into crust.
- Bake 35 – 40 minutes or until a knife inserted into the center comes out clean. Let stand for 5 to 10 minutes before serving.

Amelia Nicolson,
Care giver and companion for Hazel (Joni) Dickens

Wild Rice Quiche

9" pre-baked pie shell, cooled
1 12-ounce package Jimmy Dean sausage
1 small onion, diced
1 cup Colby-Jack cheese, shredded
1 cup long-grain and wild rice mix, cooked according to
  package instructions
3 eggs
1½ cups half and half
1/2 teaspoon salt
Dash hot pepper sauce

- Preheat oven to 350^0.
- Brown the sausage and onion until the onion is translucent. Drain.
- Sprinkle cheese on the bottom of the pie shell. Top with the sausage and onion mixture, then with the cooked long-grain and wild rice mix.
- Whip the eggs, cream, salt, pepper and hot pepper sauce together. Pour over rice.
- Bake for 50 minutes or until the center is set. Let stand for 15 minutes.
- To make in a 10" pie shell, use 5 eggs, 2 cups half and half, 1½ cups cheese, and 1½ cups cooked rice.

Kay Clarke

An Early Family's Recipe

This recipe is handed down from Imogene Clarke via her Iowa relatives. Imogene and her husband Jim, of the Harbor Springs banking family, enjoyed weekends on Lake Michigan at their place in Good Hart. Their old stone cottage, which remains in the family, was built in the early 1940s by Jim's father James Turner Clarke. It was constructed with materials at hand, large rocks brought up the dune from the shore below, and pinewood from surrounding forest. W. J. Clarke, James T. Clarke's father, was the family's first immigrant, arriving in the area from Northern Ireland via Canada in 1876.

Stuffed French Toast Casserole

SERVES 8 to 10

This recipe is great for gatherings and birthdays for kids and grandkids. Our favorite time to serve it is Christmas morning and has become a family tradition.

8 slices cubed bread without crusts
2 8-ounce packages cream cheese, cubed
12 eggs
2 cups milk
1/2 cup maple syrup
1 tablespoon cinnamon
1 tablespoon vanilla

- Gently toss bread and cream cheese into a buttered 9" x 13" baking dish.
- Whisk together the remaining ingredients and pour over the bread and cream cheese.
- Cover and refrigerate overnight.
- Preheat oven to 375⁰.
- Bake for 45 – 60 minutes.

Barbara Wibel

Joe Donatus spoons maple sugar from a burl sugar boat into molds in Good Hart.

Oven Baked French Toast

This is a great recipe to make if you have houseguests. You may prepare it the night before and bake it before breakfast. Apple Cinnamon bread from the Good Hart Store works really well for this casserole.

12 slices cinnamon or cinnamon raisin bread
2 cups half and half
2 eggs
6 tablespoons soft margarine
2 tablespoons brown sugar
2 teaspoons vanilla
1/4 teaspoon cinnamon
Berry syrup

- Preheat oven to 350^0.
- Arrange bread in 2 layers in a greased 9" x 13" baking dish.
- Blend half and half, eggs, soft margarine, brown sugar, vanilla and cinnamon and pour over bread slices.
- Press down bread until the liquid is absorbed.
- Bake for 45 minutes until the center reaches 160^0 and bread is golden brown.
- Serve hot with berry syrup.

Jaci Krieg

Lumbercamp gents take a turn at the East Hill toboggan run.

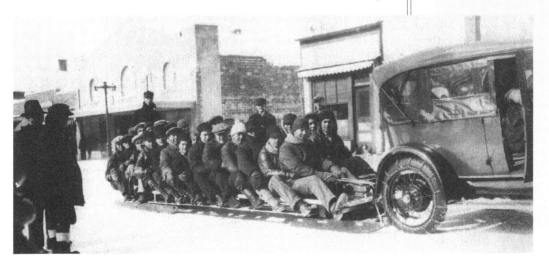

Honey

Honey and honey bees are not native to America. The bees were brought over by the colonists when they observed that the fruit trees they brought with them were not being properly pollinated. An early remedy for bee stings was made by smashing clover leaves and applying them as a poultice.

Overnight French Toast with Orange and Honey Sauce

This is very easy to prepare ahead of time and pull from the oven for breakfast especially over the holidays or when there is a big crowd at the cottage.

1/2 cup butter or margarine
1/3 cup fresh orange juice
1 tablespoon honey
4 eggs
1 loaf Vienna bread cut into 8 slices, 1" thick

SAUCE:
3/4 cup (1½ sticks) butter
1/4 cup dark brown sugar
2 tablespoons honey
1/4 teaspoon fresh lemon juice
1/4 cup fresh orange juice

- Pour 1/2 cup melted butter into a 15" x 11" jelly roll pan. Cover and refrigerate to chill.

- Whisk orange juice, honey and eggs until blended; dip bread into egg mixture and place in prepared pan. Cover and refrigerate for up to 24 hours.

- The following day, preheat the oven to 400⁰. Bake until the bottoms are golden, 8 – 10 minutes. Turn slices over and bake 7 – 8 minutes until golden brown. While toast bakes, make sauce.

- Melt 3/4 cup butter over low heat. Remove from heat; stir in brown sugar, honey, lemon juice and orange juice. Return to heat, stir to blend and reheat about 1 – 2 minutes. Serve sauce over the toast.

Janice Collins

Chipped Beef in Brown Gravy

This recipe has been in our family for over 100 years. Adding a bit of sugar and browning the flour gives a tasty twist to an old dish.

1 large or 2 small jars (2.5 ounces each) dried beef
3 tablespoons butter, divided
2 – 3 tablespoons sugar
Cracked pepper
5 tablespoons flour
1 cup water
Up to 2 cups milk

- Cut beef into bite-sized pieces. Sauté the beef in 2 tablespoons of butter in a skillet for 5 minutes over medium heat.

- Sprinkle sugar over the beef, and then add the cracked pepper to taste and stir.

- Remove the beef from the skillet and add the remaining tablespoon of butter to the skillet along with the flour. Brown the flour, stirring and scraping so it doesn't burn. Browning gives the gravy its flavor.

- Off the heat, slowly add the water and stir to avoid lumps. Return to medium heat and bring it to a slow boil, slowly add up to 2 cups of milk till the gravy has the consistency you want.

- Add the chopped beef and blend flavors.

- Serve over toast or biscuits.

- This freezes well. If you prefer less salt in the dried beef, pour boiling water over it; then drain before cooking.

Patricia Clarke

A Rock on the Shore

There's an intriguing rock along the shoreline near our Good Hart cottage, the unmistakable image of an Indian, only his head emerging from the sand — wide, firm mouth and stern brow — features etched by the ebb and flow of waves and strong west winds. He keeps watch over the dunes before him. I acknowledge him whenever I pass by; often I bow.

Some time ago, early one morning as I descended the steps to the beach, I noticed in the distance an old woman, in the company of gulls and geese, making her way among the boulders along the shore. She arrived at the rock I had found so fascinating. Apparently she, too, recognized something similar. Pausing, she stepped closer and, bending down, kissed the face on the rock.

We've been spending the summer in our cottage at the top of North Lamkin hill since 1990. It was built in 1948 where the Hilltop Cottage, a part of the Lamkin Lake Lodge, had been. It was one of the first homes that Tru Cummings built in the area and features an enormous fireplace created by Sam Keway with rocks Burt Lamkin helped haul when he was a teenager. Dale Lamkin showed us how the rocks were arranged to reflect an animal spirit. Keith and Burt Lamkin told us about dynamiting a stump in our yard and hitting a large rock that bounced off the house and just missed striking them! And a fugitive from justice once hid from the sheriff in our well pit for several days.

We remodeled in 2001, adding a screened porch where we spend much of our time and where these blintzes have been served at many fellowship coffees held after worship at Redpath Church in Cross Village where we've made so many friends over the years. Many stories about our cottage have been shared at those coffees.

Cinnamon Blintzes

This makes about seven dozen rolls that are ready to bake whenever you need them.

2 loaves sliced fluffy white bread (Inexpensive Wonder-type bread may be used.)
2 8-ounce packages cream cheese, softened
2 egg yolks
1/2 cup sugar
1 teaspoon lemon juice
1 cup firmly packed brown sugar
2 – 3 teaspoons cinnamon
1 cup butter or margarine, melted

- Trim crusts from bread. Using a rolling pin, roll the slices to flatten.

- Combine cream cheese, egg yolks, sugar and lemon juice, mixing until smooth.

- Thinly spread cream cheese mixture on bread slices and roll up.

- Combine brown sugar and cinnamon in a shallow bowl. Dip rolls in melted butter, then in brown sugar mixture and place close together on wax paper-lined baking sheets. Freeze for 5 minutes. Slice each roll in half, leaving 2 smaller rolls. Place rolls in plastic freezer bags and freeze until needed.

- Preheat oven to 350⁰. Place desired amount of frozen rolls on a greased or parchment paper lined baking sheet. Bake 10 to 15 minutes.

Trina Hayes

Mimi's Yummy Pancakes

I always double this recipe. If you don't use it all the first day, it keeps in the refrigerator for several days.

1 cup flour
1 tablespoon sugar
1 tablespoon baking powder
1 teaspoon salt
4 tablespoons sour cream
1 egg
1 cup evaporated milk
3 tablespoons melted butter

- Combine flour, sugar, baking powder and salt.
- Mix sour cream, egg and evaporated milk together and add to dry ingredients.
- Blend in 3 tablespoons melted butter.
- Cook on a hot, lightly greased or non-stick skillet or griddle.

Susan Sparrow Carson

Lamkin Lake Lodge Honeymoon

My parents honeymooned at the Lamkin Lake Shore Lodge in the 1940s. Our family continued to vacation there when my sisters and I were young. One highlight of every week's stay was the Grove Breakfast. Mrs. Lamkin had the dads cook the breakfast outdoors. Big excitement for little kids! Pancakes and eggs were cooked on the stone grills and all the guests would enjoy breakfast at the big picnic tables. I like to think Mrs. Lamkin would approve of my memories and of my pancakes!

Vere Lamkin, chef, at a Grove Breakfast

Dutch Pancake

My high school French teacher gave me this recipe. It's been a family favorite for decades since.

1 tablespoon butter or margarine
1 egg, beaten
1/4 cup flour
1/4 teaspoon salt
1/4 cup milk
Lemon
Powdered sugar

- Preheat oven to 400^0.

- Melt butter in an 8" pie or cake pan.

- Mix eggs, flour and salt into a thick paste, then gradually add the milk to make a smooth batter. Pour the batter into the cake or pie pan and bake for 20 minutes. Do not open the oven door!

- Serve immediately with lemon and powdered sugar.

- This recipe may be doubled, tripled or more to serve additional people.

Barbara Noyes-Stark

Grandma's Coffee Cake

1/4 pound butter
3/4 cup sugar
2 eggs, beaten
1 cup sour cream
1 teaspoon baking soda
1½ cups flour
1 teaspoon vanilla

TOPPING:
1/4 cup sugar
1 tablespoon cinnamon
2 tablespoons walnuts, chopped

- Preheat oven to 350⁰.
- Cream butter, 3/4 cup sugar and eggs together. Add sour cream, baking soda, flour and vanilla and mix well.
- Pour into a well-greased 9" ring pan or bundt pan.
- Combine 1/4 cup sugar, cinnamon and walnuts. Sprinkle on top of coffee cake batter and cut into cake batter before baking.
- Bake for 45 minutes. Turn over onto a plate and let set until completely cooled.

Lisa Kruzel
RFC Fire and Rescue Board Member

A Family Story

I moved to northern Michigan as a freshman in high school and graduated from Petoskey High School in 1981. After a number of years away, I moved back to Harbor Springs and we now live in Cross Village in the house my husband built.

This recipe was a staple at every family holiday as a child growing up. My mom made it for Thanksgiving and Christmas. Now I make it for my family (without nuts for the girls). I hope they will make it for their families and think of me as I think of my mom when I make it.

George Kruzel displays his record bobcat taken in the 1930s

The Cabin Tradition

Every summer Cabin Coffee Cake is anticipated by family once more returning to "The Cabin" to be enjoyed when served several times during the summer with a hearty Good Hart breakfast.

This tradition is carried on by the third generation of Ralph and Adina Foster who began building "The Cabin" 70 years ago log by log and rock by rock!

The Foster cabin, 2013

Foster's Cabin Coffee Cake

2½ cups flour
2 cups brown sugar
1/2 teaspoon salt
2/3 cup shortening
1 teaspoon cinnamon
1/2 teaspoon nutmeg
2 teaspoons baking powder
1/2 teaspoon baking soda
1¼ cups buttermilk or sour milk*
2 eggs
***To make sour milk, add 1 tablespoon vinegar to 1 cup milk and allow to set for 5 minutes.**

- Preheat oven to 350^0.
- Blend flour, brown sugar, salt and shortening until crumbly. Reserve 1/2 cup of mixture for the top of the cake. Combine the rest of the ingredients with the remaining batter and pour and spread in a greased 9" x 13" pan. Sprinkle the reserved mixture over the top of the batter.
- Bake for 30 – 35 minutes until an inserted toothpick comes out clean.

Kathleen Foster-Serra

Apple Oatmeal Coffee Cake

SERVES 9

We prepared this when fresh apples were available and the family was expecting "special" company for breakfast. It's great for fall color weekends.

1 cup all-purpose flour
3/4 teaspoon baking soda
1/2 teaspoon salt
1/4 teaspoon allspice
1/4 teaspoon cinnamon
1 cup sugar
1 cup oats
1/2 cup oil
1 egg
1 teaspoon vanilla extract
1 apple, peeled and chopped
1/3 cup nuts, chopped

- Preheat oven to 350°.
- Mix dry ingredients together in a bowl. Add remaining ingredients; the mixture will be quite thick.
- Pour into a greased 8" x 8" pan.
- Bake for 35 minutes.

Robert Smith
RFC Fire Board Member and
"Retired" Medical First Responder

SHORE DRIVE - HARBOR SPRINGS

Sour Cream Coffee Cake

1 stick butter, softened
1 cup sugar
2 eggs
1 teaspoon vanilla
2 cups flour
1 teaspoon baking soda
1 teaspoon baking powder
1/2 teaspoon salt
1 cup sour cream
TOPPING:
1/3 cup brown sugar
1/2 cup sugar
1 teaspoon cinnamon
Nuts (pecans or walnuts), crushed

- Preheat oven to 350⁰.
- Beat butter, sugar, eggs and vanilla in a mixer.
- Combine flour, baking soda, baking powder and salt in a bowl.
- Add dry ingredients to wet mixture alternating with sour cream.
- Pour half the batter into a greased 9" x 13" pan. Cover with half the topping mixture. Spoon remaining batter over the top then cover with the remaining topping mixture.
- Bake for 40 minutes.

Elizabeth McCormack
Former RFC Officer, Firefighter and EMT Specialist

Grandma's Fruity Cake

1 20-ounce can crushed pineapple, drained
1 20-ounce can blueberry, cherry, or apple pie filling
1 box dry yellow cake mix
2 sticks butter
Pecans, chopped (optional)

- Preheat oven to 350^0.
- Pour the crushed pineapple on the bottom of a greased 8½" x 11" baking dish.
- Layer blueberry (or other choice of flavor) pie filling over the pineapple.
- Sprinkle cake mix over the fruit.
- Cut sticks of butter into squares and layer on top of the cake mix layer.
- Sprinkle chopped nuts over the top.
- Bake for 44 – 55 minutes.

Janie Hess

Postcards celebrate the same curve along the Tunnel of Trees.

SHORE DRIVE
Harbor Springs, Mich.

Brunch Fruit Salad

SERVES 6
1 cup guava, cubed (optional)
2 cups fresh pineapple, cubed
1 cup orange slices
1 cup papaya, cubed
1 cup mango, cubed
1 cup strawberries, cut in half
1 cup pitted cherries
1 cup banana slices
1/4 cup macadamia nuts, halved
1/2 cup Cognac
1/2 cup Cointreau
2 tablespoons sugar
Mint sprigs

- Combine fruits and nuts.
- Mix Cognac and Cointreau with the sugar and pour over the salad. Cover and chill.
- Garnish with mint sprigs before serving.

Jane Cardinal

Fruit Dip

1 cup sour cream
3 tablespoons brown sugar
6 dry coconut macaroons, crumbled (Use the cheap ones!)
1 tablespoon rum

- Mix the sour cream, brown sugar, macaroons and rum together.
- Serve with cut fruit.

Pam O'Malley

Apple Berry Salsa with Cinnamon Chips

2 Granny Smith apples, peeled, cored and chopped
1 cup strawberries, sliced
1 kiwi, peeled and chopped
1 small orange, zest and juice or substitute orange juice
2 tablespoons apple jelly (or use any fruit jelly you prefer)

CINNAMON CHIPS:
4 flour tortillas
1 teaspoon sugar
1/2 teaspoon cinnamon

SALSA:

- Mix the fruits together with the jelly and let stand for two hours or more to blend the flavors.

TO MAKE THE CINNAMON CHIPS:

- Preheat oven to 400°.
- Mix the cinnamon and sugar together.
- Moisten the tortillas with water and sprinkle with the sugar mixture. Cut each tortilla into 8 wedges.
- Bake for 8 to 10 minutes or until lightly browned and crisp.
- Serve cinnamon chips with apple berry salsa.

Laura Ward

Good Hart Cooler

Hibiscus tea and lemonade make a beautiful red Good Hart version of an Arnold Palmer that's herbal and naturally without caffeine.

Minute Maid frozen lemonade concentrate
1 tablespoon hibiscus tea
2 cups water

- Make lemonade according to directions on the Minute Maid can.
- Heat 2 cups water and brew 1 tablespoon of hibiscus tea (available at the Good Hart and Soul Tea Room) for 5 to 8 minutes. Cool.
- Add lemonade according to taste.

Good Hart and Soul Tea Room

Hot Cider Punch

This has kept us warm at many football tailgate brunches.

6 cups apricot nectar
6 cups apple juice
6 tablespoons sugar
6 tablespoons lemon juice
10 whole cloves

- Combine all ingredients and bring to a boil, stirring until the sugar is dissolved.
- The flavor is improved if this is refrigerated for a day or two then reheated in a crock pot or coffee urn.
- Apple brandy or other "spirits" of your choice may be added to individual servings.

Trina Hayes

Memorial Punch

SERVES 24

This punch is used for receptions after funerals and memorial services at my winter church, Flossmoor Community Church in Illinois. It's tasty for all occasions.

1 quart pineapple sherbet
1 quart vanilla ice cream
24 ounces pineapple juice
36 ounces lemon-lime soda (7-Up, Sprite or other)

- Mix all ingredients in a punch bowl.

Trina Hayes

Holiday Punch

Everyone likes this at Christmas because it's lighter than eggnog.

1 gallon French vanilla ice cream, softened (We use Breyer's)
3 cups brandy
1 gallon skim milk
Nutmeg to taste

- Combine softened ice cream and brandy in a punch bowl and freeze.
- Just before serving, slowly stir the skim milk into the frozen ice cream and brandy mixture. Add nutmeg to taste.

Trina Hayes

The Native Americans of L'Arbre Croche traveled to winter hunting camps on or near the Muskegon River. Winter hunting was tedious as game had to be stalked down wind. The average range of an arrow was 125 feet, so that meant getting as close to prey as possible. One amazing feat involved what was called the "mortar shot" in which an arrow was shot directly skyward to strike a specific target on the ground. Typically ten arrows could be released by the archer before the first struck the target.

Recipe For:_____

_____

_____

_____

_____

_____

_____

_____

_____

_____

_____

_____

_____

_____

_____

_____

_____

_____

_____

_____

_____

_____

_____

_____

_____

_____

_____

_____

_____

_____

_____

_____

_____

_____

_____

Salads & Dressings

Devil's Elbow in Winter, 1951, by Virgil D. Haynes
©Haynes Studio, Harbor Springs

Recipes

Genuine German Potato Salad

SERVES 8 to 10

We serve this family favorite for the Fourth of July and other holidays. It has a very mild and different flavor.

10 medium potatoes
1 small onion, thinly sliced
1 tablespoon oil
2 teaspoons salt
1/2 teaspoon pepper
2½ tablespoons vinegar
4 tablespoons mayonnaise (Use real mayonnaise like Hellmann's.)
2 tablespoons milk
1/2 tablespoon water

- Cook potatoes in boiling salted water until tender, about 20 minutes. Drain and cool completely. Peel potatoes and slice thinly.

- Gently mix potato and onion slices together.

- Thoroughly mix the oil, salt, pepper, vinegar, mayonnaise, milk and water together.

- Pour dressing mixture over the potato and onion mixture.

- Let sit for 30 minutes before refrigerating overnight. Serve cold.

Susan Sponseller

The Good Hart beach, a 1940s photo by Cliff Powers

Dilled Potato and Pickled Cucumber Salad

This salad has many steps but it's worth it. The pickled cucumbers are also great on their own. Find the fresh dill at Pond Hill Farm north of Harbor Springs and Bill's Farm Market outside Petoskey.

6 tablespoons distilled white vinegar
4 teaspoons coarse kosher salt
2 16-ounce English cucumbers, very thinly sliced
1/2 cup plus 3 tablespoons chopped fresh dill
3¼ pounds Yukon Gold potatoes (about 10 medium)
Additional kosher salt
Pepper, coarsely ground, to taste
1 cup white onion, very thinly sliced
2 – 3 green onions, thinly sliced, white parts only
8 radishes, thinly sliced
3/8 cup mayonnaise
3/8 cup sour cream
Small radishes with tops for garnish
Salt and pepper to taste

- Stir vinegar and 4 teaspoons of coarse kosher salt together in a small bowl until the salt dissolves. Place cucumbers and 1/2 cup of dill in a heavy 1-gallon resealable plastic bag. Add the vinegar mixture; seal the bag. Turn several times to coat. Refrigerate overnight, turning the bag occasionally.

- Pour cucumber mixture into a large sieve set over a bowl. Drain for at least 1 hour and up to 3 hours. Discard the brine.

- Cook potatoes in a large pot of boiling salted water until tender, about 30 minutes. Drain. Cool potatoes completely. Peel potatoes; quarter lengthwise (if using medium potatoes). Cut crosswise into 1/2-inch thick slices. Place potatoes in a large bowl and sprinkle generously with coarse kosher salt and pepper.

- Add drained cucumbers, onions, radishes and the remaining 3 tablespoons dill; toss to blend.

- Let stand 1 hour. Mix sour cream and mayonnaise together and stir into the salad. Season generously with salt and pepper, if desired.

- Cover and refrigerate. This salad may be made one day ahead.

- Mound the salad in a bowl; garnish with small whole radishes. Serve cold or at room temperature.

Sandy Kasischke

Historic Location

Our family has owned the property at our current location on Lamkin Road since 1946. My mother believed our lot was the location of the original Native American church in the area, because of a foundation and artifacts found during the construction of our house in 1951.

Hot Potato Salad

SERVES 10 to 12
7-8 large potatoes, cooked and cubed
1/2 pound bacon, cut into 1-inch pieces
1 medium onion, sliced or diced, to taste
1/2 cup celery, diced into pieces, to taste
1 small green pepper, diced
1¾ cups mayonnaise
1/4 cup cider vinegar
2 – 3 tablespoons sugar

- Cook the bacon in a skillet until crisp. Remove and drain.
- Reserve 2-3 tablespoons of bacon fat in the skillet.
- Add onion, celery and green pepper to the reserved bacon fat and cook until tender.
- Mix mayonnaise, vinegar and sugar with a wire whisk in a small bowl or 2-cup measuring cup. Adjust the sugar to your taste.
- Pour mixture into the hot skillet over the vegetables.
- Add reserved bacon pieces and stir well.
- Immediately pour the bacon mixture over the warm cubed potatoes.
- Serve warm.

Caroline Smith Lewis

A Celebrity Chef offering . . . the Goodmans

Salad Nicoise

Prepare this one-dish meal in advance so you'll be able to spend time with your guests. Adjust the portions to fit the size of your crowd.

1 yellow fin tuna steak
Redskin potatoes, miniature size, boiled
Green beans, steamed (crisp)
Grape tomatoes
Nicoise olives (pitted)
Vinaigrette dressing
Olive oil
Black pepper, coarsely ground
Eggs, hard cooked

- Coat yellow fin tuna steak with olive oil and coarsely ground black pepper. Grill tuna to medium rare.

- Toss potatoes, green beans, tomatoes and olives in your favorite vinaigrette.

- Slice tuna and serve atop salad ingredients on a large platter.

- Arrange eggs as garnish.

Greg and Susan Goodman
Café Bon Homme

For more than two decades, current Good Hart residents Greg and Susan Goodman owned the prestigious Café Bon Homme in Plymouth, Michigan, where Greg was also the chef. Highly regarded for its contemporary European cuisine, the restaurant was featured in publications including Gourmet and Bon Appetit. Bon Homme is the French translation of "good man" — thus it was the perfect name for the Goodman's café.

Redskin Potato Salad

SERVES 12

This recipe is dedicated to Cedric Richner III.

2 – 3 pounds redskin potatoes
1/2 cup onion, chopped (optional)
3/4 cup sour cream
3/4 cup mayonnaise
1/4 cup white vinegar
1 tablespoon Dijon mustard
1 teaspoon salt
1½ teaspoon pepper
1/2 cup fresh dill
2 eggs, hard-boiled and sliced

- Boil potatoes; drain and cool. Cut cooled potatoes into cubes.
- Mix remaining ingredients, except eggs.
- Stir onion in with dressing mixture, if desired.
- Add dressing mixture to potatoes and blend.
- Garnish with sliced eggs and dill.

Susan Richner

The Chingwa is the 150-year-old Richner cottage in Middle Village. Photo by Kathy Hannah

French Potato Salad with Bacon

SERVES 4
1 pound (8 or 9) new potatoes
1/4 pound bacon
1/4 cup shallots, finely chopped
1/4 cup red wine vinegar
2 tablespoons olive oil
Salt and freshly ground pepper to taste
1/4 cup purple onion, chopped
1/2 cup parsley, chopped

- Scrub potatoes under running water with a soft brush. Quarter potatoes and drop into a pot of cold, salted water. Bring to a boil and cook until tender but still firm, about 8 to 10 minutes after the water reaches a boil.

- Chop bacon and sauté in a small skillet until crisp. Remove bacon and reserve.

- In the remaining bacon fat, sauté the chopped shallots until tender, about 5 minutes. Reserve shallots and fat.

- When potatoes are cooked, drain and place them in a large mixing bowl.

- Pour vinegar, olive oil, shallots and reserved bacon fat over the still-hot potatoes. Season with salt and pepper to taste and gently toss.

- Add the purple onion and parsley and toss again.

- Cool to room temperature, cover and refrigerate.

- Before serving, bring back to room temperature, toss, correct seasoning and add additional oil and vinegar if the salad seems dry.

- Sprinkle reserved crisp bacon on top.

Kay Clarke

Macaroni Salad

MAKES 2 QUARTS
2 cups uncooked macaroni
2 cups frozen peas, cooked till just tender and drained
3 eggs, hard boiled, chopped
Ranch dressing of your choice, enough to moisten
1 cup (or 1 can) Albacore tuna or diced chicken
1 medium onion, chopped
1 small to medium can black olives, sliced
3-4 dill pickles, sliced
Salt and pepper to taste

- Cook macaroni according to package directions.
- Add peas and eggs to macaroni.
- Add enough ranch dressing to moisten.
- Mix in the rest of the ingredients and add salt and pepper to taste.
- Refrigerate to cool.

Deborah Root

Main Street, Cross Village, before the 1918 fire — at one time Cross Village was the largest settlement in Michigan.

Spinach Pasta Salad

SERVES 10 to 12

I shared this recipe with my mother after serving it at a family reunion. I later discovered it in her recipe box after she passed away.

8 ounces of spinach corkscrew pasta, cooked, drained and rinsed
1 8-ounce can artichoke hearts (packed in water), drained and cut into small pieces
3/4 cup ripe olives, pitted and sliced
1 4-ounce jar sliced pimento
1 medium red onion, chopped
1 ounce provolone cheese, cubed
1 ounce cheddar cheese, cubed
1/3 cup white wine vinegar
1/4 cup salad oil
2 tablespoons honey
3/4 teaspoon crushed dried basil
1/2 teaspoon dried dill weed
1/2 teaspoon garlic powder
1/2 teaspoon pepper
1/4 teaspoon salt

- Combine the pasta, artichoke hearts, olives, pimento, onion and cheeses in a large bowl and toss to mix.

- Combine remaining ingredients in a screw-top jar and shake well. Pour over pasta and toss to coat. Refrigerate several hours or overnight to mingle flavors.

Debbie Dicken

Postcard photo by Dale Lamkin

A Celebrity Chef offering . . . Bob Vala

Crow's Nest Chicken Salad

4 cups mixed greens
2 tablespoons dried cherries
2 tablespoons walnuts, chopped
4 tomato wedges
2 ounces Boursin cheese, crumbled
1 5-ounce chicken breast, cooked and chopped

- Combine the mixed greens on a dinner plate. Arrange dried cherries, walnuts, tomato wedges, crumbled Boursin cheese and chicken over the greens.
- Serve with 1/4 cup of the balsamic vinaigrette (recipe follows) either on the side or toss it with the mixed greens before topping with the remaining ingredients.

BALSAMIC VINAIGRETTE
1/4 cup Dijon mustard
1/4 cup sugar
1/2 cup balsamic vinegar
3/4 tablespoon salt or to taste
3/4 tablespoon pepper or to taste
1½ tablespoons dried basil
1 tablespoon brown sugar
2 cups olive oil

- Mix mustard, sugar, vinegar, salt, pepper, basil and brown sugar together well.
- Slowly add the olive oil while continuing to mix.

Bob Vala
Chef and Owner, *The Crow's Nest*

"I grew up on the eastside of Detroit and spent my summers on Mullet Lake. I started cooking at the age of six. My grandmothers were Italian and Hungarian and my mother was a very talented cook. I was the youngest in a family of six. I often cooked dinner for the whole family since both my parents worked. My first cooking job was at Ellis Brothers, then I worked at the Fox and Hounds and Win Shuler's. When I was 23, I decided to get serious about becoming a chef. I headed to the Culinary Institute of America in Hyde Park, New York.

"After attending cooking school for two years, my wife Anne and I moved to northern Michigan. My first job was as Executive Chef at Stafford's Pier in Harbor Springs. After ten years I was given the job as Food and Beverage Director at the Perry Hotel.

"In 1995, friends Dee and Steve Serva took Ann and me to dinner at the Crow's Nest and introduced us to owners Mike and Linda McElroy. Although she was kidding at the time, Dee told the McElroys that Ann and I would be the next owners of the restaurant. Two years later Mike and Linda sold to us, and we've owned the Crow's Nest since 1997."

Bob Vala

Pine Nut Salad

The colors in this salad are perfect at Christmas.

Romaine lettuce, torn into bite-sized pieces
1 red bell pepper, chopped
1 yellow pepper, chopped
1 bunch green onions, sliced
1 and 1/2 cups feta cheese, crumbled
1/3 cup fresh dill
1 and 1/3 cups toasted pine nuts
8 ounces of cherry or grape tomatoes, halved
1 14-ounce can sliced beets, drained

DRESSING:
1 tablespoon balsamic vinegar
1 tablespoon rcd wine vinegar
1 teaspoon Dijon mustard
A pinch of tarragon
Minced garlic to taste, optional
5 tablespoons olive oil
Salt and pepper to taste

- Mix romaine, peppers, onions, feta cheese, dill and pine nuts in a large bowl.
- Fold in the tomatoes and sliced beets.
- Mix vinegars, mustard, tarragon and garlic. Whisk in the olive oil and add salt and pepper to taste.
- Toss the dressing with the salad.
- Don't skimp on the pine nuts — the secret ingredient.

Susan Carson

Looking north at the Lamkin dunes

A calendar photo by Cliff Powers

Harvest Salad

1 bag Italian Salad mix
1 bag chopped romaine hearts
2 cups Swiss cheese, shredded
1 tart green apple, peeled and cut in chunks
1 ripe pear, peeled and cut in chunks
1 cup dried cranberries
1 cup cashews
Brianna's brand Poppy Seed Dressing (or make your own)

- Mix the first 7 ingredients together and toss with poppy seed dressing.

Gail Selvala

Blue Cheese and Bacon Salad

SERVES 6 to 8

SALAD MIXTURE:
Lettuce, including some iceberg, chopped
Tomatoes, chopped
Purple onions, sliced
Blue cheese crumbles
Bacon, cooked, drained and chopped

DRESSING:
1/4 cup oil
1/3 cup white vinegar
1/3 cup sugar
2 teaspoons salt

- Toss lettuce, tomatoes and purple onion slices together.
- Mix dressing ingredients and right before serving, toss the salad mixture with dressing.
- Top with blue cheese crumbles and chopped bacon.

Patricia Clarke

St. Ignatius School was established in Middle Village in the early 1800s.

"Other Side of the Lake" Spinach Salad

1 pound spinach, washed, stemmed and dried
8 slices bacon, cooked crisply and crumbled
3 eggs, hard boiled and diced

DRESSING:
1 cup salad oil
3/4 cup sugar
1/3 cup catsup
1/4 cup cider vinegar
1 teaspoon Worcestershire Sauce
1 small onion, grated or 1 tablespoon dry minced onion
Salt to taste

- Mix spinach, bacon and eggs in a large bowl.
- Pour dressing ingredients in a screw-top jar and shake until well mixed.
- Pour about 3/4 cup of the dressing over the salad mixture and toss till coated. Add more dressing if desired.
- The dressing will keep for several days and makes enough for at least 2 salads.

Larry Hayes

Baby Spinach and Coleslaw

1 cup sugared pecans (see below)
1 egg white
Cinnamon sugar mix in shaker jar or make your own
1 16-ounce bag of baby spinach, cut in pieces
1 16-ounce bag coleslaw mix
1 cup dried cranberries or cherries
1 bottle Ken's Sweet Vidalia Onion Dressing or use your
own recipe

- Preheat oven to 300^0.

- Toss 1 cup pecans with 1 egg white in a plastic bag. Coat well.

- Place the pecans on a baking sheet and sprinkle them with cinnamon sugar mixture.

- Bake for 20 minutes. Allow to cool.

- Mix spinach, coleslaw mix, dried cranberries or cherries and sugared pecans.

- Add dressing (amount as desired) and toss till coated.

Gail Selvala

The Harbor Point Light was served by Elizabeth Whitney Williams when it was built in 1884.

Bluff Gardens

Bluff Gardens began as a farm stand on Lake Shore Drive just north of Harbor Springs in 1934. Sophie Carpenter and her family grew and sold miniature vegetables there. Their vegetable gardens and store moved to Lake Street in the 1990s. Betty Little got this recipe from Sophie many years ago.

Sophie's Coleslaw

2 pounds chopped cabbage
1 small onion, chopped
1 green pepper, chopped

DRESSING:
3/4 cup oil
3/4 cup vinegar
1 cup sugar
1 teaspoon salt
1/2 teaspoon celery salt

- Mix all dressing ingredients in a pot and bring to a boil and cook until combined.
- Mix cabbage, onion and green pepper in a large bowl.
- Pour hot dressing over vegetables.
- Cool and store covered in the refrigerator for 24 hours before serving.
- This will keep in the refrigerator for several weeks.

Sophie Carpenter
via Betty Little's recipe box

A Heritage Recipe . . .

Maree Baxter's Salad

2 parts grated cabbage
1 part grated carrots
1 part ground salted peanuts

- Mix all ingredients together with any desired mayonnaise or salad dressing.

Jo Cunningham

The Pebble

Maree and her husband, Fred, spent two weeks at the Pebble each summer from 1930 to 1950. They rented the cottage from Agnes Hulbert of Detroit. Maree kept a daily diary from age 12 until she died in 1958. She often wrote about serving this salad to guests. It was also a favorite of her grandson, Fred, who now is the owner of the Pebble.

Clarke Coleslaw

SERVES 10 to 12
5 cups cabbage, shredded
1/2 cup almonds, toasted
1½ cups dried cranberries
1/2 cup celery, diced
1/2 cup green onions, white and green parts, chopped
1/2 cup green bell pepper, chopped

DRESSING:
1/2 cup mayonnaise
1 tablespoon sweet pickle relish
1 tablespoon honey mustard
1 tablespoon honey
Salt and pepper to taste

- Combine cabbage, almonds, cranberries, celery, green onions and green pepper in a large plastic bowl with a snap on lid or in a non-metallic bowl covered tightly.

- Combine all dressing ingredients, adding salt and pepper to taste, and refrigerate until ready to serve.

- Pour dressing over slaw just before serving. Stir well.

Susan Clarke

An early Clarke cottage under construction in Middle Village

Marie Smith's Molded Cabbage Salad

1 3-ounce package lime gelatin
1 cup boiling water
1/2 cup cold water
2/3 cup mayonnaise
3/4 teaspoon salt
2 teaspoons vinegar
2 tablespoons onion, grated
3/4 teaspoon celery seed
2 cups cabbage, shredded

- Mix the gelatin with boiling water then add cold water.
- With a mixer, blend in the mayonnaise and then add the remaining ingredients.
- Pour into a 7½" by 12" dish and chill until the gelatin sets.

Rosemary Stolt

A Church Potluck

Jim and Marie Smith hosted a potluck lunch at their home for the congregation of the First Presbyterian Church in Harbor Springs in the 1970s. It was so much fun playing all kinds of games and visiting in their spacious yard. Marie made this Molded Cabbage Salad for the occasion and she shared the recipe with me. It's different from most gelatin salads in that it is not so sweet.

Broccoli Slaw

1 large bag broccoli slaw
1 package Oriental Ramen Noodles
1/2 cup green onions, chopped
1/2 cup green pepper, chopped
1/2 cup red pepper, chopped
1 small package (about 1/3 cup) slivered almonds
1 small package (about 1/2 cup) sunflower seeds
1/2 cup dried cranberries or cherries

DRESSING:
2/3 cup canola oil
2/3 cup sugar
1/3 cup white vinegar

- Open the package of ramen noodles; set aside the seasoning packet.

- In a large bowl, mix together the broccoli slaw, onions and chopped green and red peppers. Break up the ramen noodles into small pieces and toss thoroughly over all.

- Mix the dressing ingredients in a small bowl until the sugar dissolves.

- Pour over the slaw mixture and mix well.

- Refrigerate for at least 2 hours.

- Just before serving add the slivered almonds, sunflower seeds and dried cranberries or cherries.

Kathy Hannah

Going to the blueberry camp

Summer Tomatoes

Our family always looks forward to those very special up north August meals of freshly picked corn and tomatoes. We have a serving platter piled high with grilled or boiled corn and a big plate of summer tomatoes. That's it! No meat, no bread, no other vegetables, just lots of corn and tomatoes. They're especially good if picked that day.

DRESSING:
3 tablespoons extra-virgin olive oil
2 tablespoons cider vinegar
3/4 teaspoon packed light brown sugar
1/3 teaspoon salt (fleur de sel, if available)
1/3 teaspoon coarsely ground pepper

SALAD:
2 pounds ripe tomatoes, cut in 1/2" slices (Use ripe, fresh, beefsteak, heirloom or cherry tomatoes — make sure they are ripe!)
1 scallion, white and green parts, thinly sliced
Fresh dill
Fresh parsley

- Whisk together the oil, vinegar, brown sugar, salt and pepper in a small bowl.
- Arrange a third of the sliced tomatoes in 1 layer on a plate and drizzle with the dressing.
- Make 2 more layers of tomatoes, drizzling each layer with dressing.
- You can make this up to 6 hours before serving and cover and chill in the refrigerator. Try to do it just before serving though so you won't have to chill the fresh tomatoes.
- Sprinkle with sliced scallions just before serving.
- Serve with fresh dill and parsley to sprinkle on individual servings.
- Serve any extra dressing at the table.

Carolyn Shear

Cucumber Salad

SERVES 6 to 8

2 – 3 cucumbers, thinly sliced (Peel if using regular cucumbers but leave the peel on English cucumbers – the long skinny ones.)

Parsley

MARINADE:

1/2 cup sugar

1/2 cup white vinegar

1/2 teaspoon salt

2 tablespoons parsley or chives

- Dissolve the sugar and salt in the vinegar.
- Add the thinly sliced cucumbers and 2 tablespoons chopped parsley or chives.
- Chill. Drain before serving and garnish with parsley.
- This is best made in the morning and served later in the day but it is acceptable for 2 to 3 days.

Mary Curzan

Juniper Lodge, childhood cottage of Mary Curzan

New West Salsa Salad

2 cups plum tomatoes, chopped
1/2 mango, chopped
1 cup Granny Smith apples, chopped
1/2 cup cucumber, chopped
1/2 cup fresh corn kernels
1/2 cup red pepper, chopped
1/4 cup green onions, sliced
1 package edemame beans
2½ tablespoons fresh cilantro, chopped

DRESSING:
1½ tablespoons fresh lime juice
1 tablespoon balsamic vinegar
1½ teaspoons sugar
3/4 teaspoon salt
1/2 teaspoon freshly ground pepper

- Combine all vegetables and cilantro in a large bowl.
- Stir dressing ingredients together and pour over vegetables.
- Stir well and serve at room temperature or chilled.

Linda Dibble

Spicy Kale and Carrot Salad with Nuts

We built our cabin on the site of the old Lamkin apple orchards and reserved land for a vegetable garden. Kale particularly loves the fertile soil.

1 cup dry roasted unsalted peanuts, chopped*
1 large bunch of kale, shredded**
1-2 tablespoons sesame oil
5-6 carrots, grated
1 bunch of green onions or fresh chives, finely chopped
1/2 cup roasted unsalted sunflower seeds
1/2 cup raw pumpkin seeds
2 tablespoons Thai sweet chili sauce
1/2 – 1 teaspoon chili garlic sauce (found in the Asian section of most grocery stores)
1/2 – 2/3 cup Newman's Own Low Fat Sesame Ginger dressing

*The amount and type of nuts can be adjusted. I have also used toasted sesame seeds and toasted sliced almonds.
**Use regular kale, red kale or Lacinato kale.

- Chop the peanuts in a food processor then place them in a large bowl.
- Wash and drain the kale. Remove the tough center stalks.
- Add the kale, a few large handfuls at a time, to the processor and pulse to shred.
- Place the kale in the bowl with the peanuts and drizzle with the sesame oil.
- Using the shredder blade process the carrots.
- Add the shredded carrots and the remaining ingredients to the kale and peanuts.
- Toss with the salad dressing to your taste.

Sue Kleo

Copper Pennies

SERVES 8
2 pounds carrots, sliced on the diagonal, about 1/4-inch thick
1 large white onion, chopped
1 green pepper, chopped
SAUCE:
1/2 cup sugar
1 can tomato soup
1/4 cup white vinegar
1/4 cup salad oil
1/2 teaspoon dry mustard
1/4 teaspoon pepper
1/2 teaspoon salt

- Bring a pot of water to a boil and add the carrots cooking them for 7 to 8 minutes until just tender. Drain and let cool.

- Mix sauce ingredients while the carrots cool.

- Pour sauce mixture over cooled carrots and mix in chopped onions and green pepper.

- Cover and refrigerate for 24 hours.

- This keeps for several days.

Carolyn Shear

The "Emmas' Pennies"

This is great picnic fare and always seems to be a hit. It was a favorite dish served every year at our family reunions on Lake Huron. We called it "the Emmas' Pennies" because all of our Emmas (two great aunts and my grandmother) made this every year on the first day of the reunion. They enlisted all of the grandchildren to peel the carrots, and we cousins had contests to see who could make the longest peel. When we finished, the Emmas would declare the carrot peel winner (all of us!) and begin to slice the "pennies."

It seemed to us kids that the Emmas lived on the screened kitchen porch — snapping beans, handing out peas in the pod, or better — cookies, talking, laughing, and always, always making something good to eat.

A Celebrity Chef offering . . . Susan Goodman

Roasted Vegetables with Orzo Salad

We are relative newcomers to the area, having bought our cabin in 2002 and moving here full-time in 2008. However, our family has a long history of "cottage-ing" on the Canadian shore of Lake Huron. When my dad and grandfather died and the cottage was sold, we were anxious to reestablish the family tradition. The Good Hart-Cross Village area has captured our hearts and we now enjoy the same family gatherings of years past including bonfires and endless games of croquet!

SALAD:
1 small eggplant, peeled and diced
1 red pepper, diced
1 yellow pepper, diced
1 red onion, peeled and diced
2 cloves garlic, minced
1/3 cup olive oil
1/2 teaspoon kosher salt
1/2 teaspoon freshly ground black pepper
1/2 pound orzo pasta

DRESSING:
1/3 cup freshly squeezed lemon juice
1/3 cup olive oil
1 teaspoon kosher salt
1/2 teaspoon freshly ground pepper

TOPPING:
4 scallions, minced
1/4 cup pine nuts, roasted
3/4 pound feta cheese, diced
15 fresh basil leaves, cut into chiffonade

- Preheat oven to 425⁰.

- Toss eggplant, peppers, onion, garlic, oil, salt and pepper together on a large baking sheet and roast for 40 minutes, turning once with a spatula.

- While the vegetables are roasting, cook the orzo in boiling salted water for 7 – 9 minutes.

- Drain and transfer the orzo to a large serving bowl.

- Add the roasted vegetables to the orzo including the scraps and all liquid and seasonings into the bowl.

- Make the dressing by combining the lemon juice, olive oil, salt and pepper. Pour over the orzo pasta and vegetables.

- Let cool to room temperature then add scallions, pine nuts, feta and basil.

- Serve at room temperature.

Susan Goodman
Café Bon Homme

Helen Gablo of Middle Village

Photo by Cliff Powers

Chickpea Salad with Cilantro Dressing

SERVES 6

When asked to bring a salad for a potluck, I use this recipe because it can be made in advance. It's perfect for busy people.

1 cup seeded, peeled cucumber, chopped
3/4 cup radishes, thinly sliced
3/4 cup celery, chopped
2 15½-ounce cans chickpeas (garbanzo beans), rinsed and drained
1/2 cup green onions, chopped
12 Boston lettuce leaves

DRESSING:
2 cups fresh cilantro, chopped
2 tablespoons extra virgin olive oil
1/2 teaspoon lime rind, grated
2 tablespoons fresh lime juice
1/8 teaspoon salt
2 garlic cloves, chopped or mashed
3-4 pickled jalapeno pepper slices (from a can or jar)
1/4 cup fat-free less sodium chicken broth

- Make dressing by combining cilantro, olive oil, lime rind, lime juice, salt, garlic cloves and jalapeno pepper slices in a food processor or blender. Process until well blended. Add chicken broth; pulse until combined.

- Combine cucumber, radishes, celery and chickpeas in a large bowl.

- Drizzle with cilantro mixture; toss to coat.

- At this point you may refrigerate until needed.

- To serve, arrange lettuce leaves on a platter, spoon chickpea mixture over lettuce.

Irene Hammill

A Heritage Recipe . . .

Five Bean Salad

1 can cut green beans, well drained
1 can cut yellow beans, well drained
1 can ceci (garbanzo) beans, well drained
1 can small lima beans, well drained
1 can kidney beans, well drained
1 medium onion, chopped finely
1 cup celery, chopped
1 green pepper, chopped (optional)
Salt

MARINADE:
1 cup oil
1 cup sugar
1 cup white vinegar

- Mix oil, sugar and white vinegar together.
- Mix all vegetables together.
- Pour marinade over the vegetables; salt to taste.
- Cover and marinate overnight.

Nellie Powers
via Betty Little's recipe box

Cliff and Nellie Powers' grocery store and gas station in winter

Black Bean and Corn Salad

2 cans black beans, drained and rinsed
2 cups frozen corn kernels
Minced garlic to taste
1/2 cup onion, finely chopped
1 green bell pepper, finely chopped

DRESSING:
1/2 teaspoon salt
1/4 cup olive oil
1/4 cup lime juice
1/2 cup cilantro, chopped
1/2 cup parsley, chopped
1/4 – 1/2 teaspoon red pepper flakes

- Combine beans, corn, garlic, onion and green pepper in a large bowl.
- Mix all dressing ingredients in a small bowl; pour over bean mixture and stir to mix.

Kira Stolen

Black Bean Confetti Salad

2 15-ounce cans black beans, rinsed and drained
1 small red pepper, finely diced
4 scallions, thinly sliced
2 tablespoons fresh cilantro, chopped
2 tablespoons white wine vinegar
1 tablespoon extra virgin olive oil

- In a large glass bowl, combine the beans, diced pepper, scallions, cilantro, vinegar and oil. Stir well to combine.

- Let stand for 15 minutes.

- You can prepare this up to a day in advance.

- Cover and refrigerate. Bring to room temperature before serving.

Carolyn Shear

The washout at Talbot Beach, 1924

Pineapple Gelatin Salad

SERVES 6 to 8
1 3-ounce package lime-flavored gelatin
1 cup hot water
1 cup pineapple syrup
1/4 cup sugar, if desired
1 cup crushed pineapple
1 cup cottage cheese
1/2 cup broken walnuts
1 cup heavy whipping cream, whipped (or substitute mayonnaise)

- Soften the gelatin in hot water.
- Add the pineapple syrup and sugar if desired and refrigerate until partially set.
- Add pineapple, cottage cheese and nuts.
- Fold in whipped cream or mayonnaise.
- Turn into a 1-quart mold. Chill.

Sally Lamkin

Solomon Francis and Dale Lamkin, 1985

Cranberry Salad

1 3-ounce package raspberry gelatin
3/4 cup boiling water
3/4 cup orange juice
10 ounces (1/2 a 20-ounce can) crushed pineapple,
    drained
1 can whole berry cranberry sauce
1/2 cup chopped walnuts

- Dissolve gelatin in boiling water.
- Add orange juice; chill until thickened.
- Add pineapple, cranberry sauce and walnuts.
- Pour into a mold or dish and chill until firm.

Bonnie Bliss Weitzel

Becky's Cranberry Salad

2 3-ounce packages lemon gelatin
2 cups boiling water
1 can whole berry cranberry sauce
1/2 cup crushed pineapple, drained
1/2 cup chopped walnuts or other nuts of your choice

- Mix gelatin with boiling water to dissolve.
- Stir in the cranberry sauce and heat until smooth.
- Add pineapple and walnuts.
- Pour into an 8" by 8" square pan or small mold and
  chill until set.

The Wortley Family

Shore Drive Club

The women in our local Shore Drive Study Club get together regularly throughout the year and I have often served this salad which they enjoy. I also make desserts for them from my mother Dorothy's recipes. Do you suppose ladies ate the same dishes when Dorothy Bliss belonged to the club, when it was called the Shore Drive Extension Club?

Reception Salad

SERVES 6 to 8

This salad was served to guests at the Lamkin Lodge in Good Hart in the 1950s.

6 ounces of cream cheese
1 small jar chopped pimento
1 3-ounce package lemon gelatin
Pineapple juice from one large can crushed pineapple;
  reserve pineapple
1/4 – 1/2 cup celery, finely diced
1/2 cup walnut meats, fairly finely diced
1/2 pint whipping cream, whipped (or 1 package
    Dream Whip, prepared according to directions)
1/8 teaspoon salt

- Mix cream cheese with pimento and reserved crushed pineapple. Set aside.

- Add pineapple juice to the lemon gelatin; boil the juice and gelatin together.

- When the gelatin mixture begins to set, add all the other ingredients.

- Pour into individual molds or in a ring mold and chill until thoroughly set.

Nancy Buskirk

Lamkin Lake Shore Lodge – this 1936 Lodge replaced two prior lodges that burned

Coleslaw Dressing

1/2 teaspoon salt
1/2 teaspoon onion powder
Freshly ground pepper
1 tablespoon basil vinegar
3 tablespoons oil

- Mix all ingredients together.

Betty Little

Lettuce Salad Dressing

1/2 teaspoon salt
1/2 teaspoon Beau Monde spice
1 teaspoon onion powder
1/4 teaspoon salad herbs
1½ tablespoons vinegar
4½ tablespoons oil

- Mix all ingredients together.

Betty Little

Fruit Salad Dressing

2/3 cup sugar
1/4 teaspoon salt
1 teaspoon dry mustard
1 teaspoon celery seed
1 teaspoon paprika
3 tablespoons cider vinegar
1 tablespoon lemon juice
1/2 teaspoon onion, grated
1 cup vegetable oil
1/3 cup honey

- Combine sugar, salt, mustard, celery seed and paprika.
- Blend in vinegar, lemon juice and onion.
- Gradually add oil, whisking to blend.
- Add honey and blend well.

Trina Hayes

Soups & Stews

The beach at Good Hart/Middle Village, 1950s, by Cliff Powers

Recipes

Tortellini and Spinach Soup

SERVES 4

1 10-ounce package frozen chopped spinach
1 teaspoon olive oil
3/4 cup onion, chopped
1 teaspoon bottled minced garlic
2 cups water
2 14½-ounce cans fat-free roasted garlic-seasoned
   chicken broth (or substitute plain chicken broth)
1 14-ounce can chopped tomatoes
1 teaspoon sugar, optional
1 9-ounce package portabella mushroom tortellini or
   the tortellini of your choice
3 tablespoons Parmesan cheese, shredded
1/4 teaspoon ground black pepper
1/4 teaspoon salt
1 egg

- Defrost spinach. Sauté garlic and onion in the olive oil until the onion is tender.

- Add water and broth to garlic and onion and bring to a boil. Next add well-drained spinach, tomatoes with juice and tortellini. Bring to a boil then reduce heat to a slow boil. Cook for 5 minutes.

- Whisk cheese, salt, pepper and egg together. Slowly drizzle egg mixture into soup. Stir and cook constantly for 2 minutes.

Marge Edwards

Light Gazpacho

6 large tomatoes, diced with seeds and juice
1 medium red onion, chopped
3/4 cucumber, peeled and chopped
1½ yellow or orange pepper, chopped
1/2 cup cilantro, chopped
2 tablespoons red wine vinegar
Juice from 1/2 a lemon or 1/2 a lime
1/2 tablespoon Worcestershire Sauce
1/2 tablespoon Tabasco
Kosher salt to taste
Pepper to taste
1/4 cup extra-virgin olive oil
Balsamic vinegar
Light sour cream

- Mix tomatoes, onion, cucumber, pepper, cilantro, red wine vinegar, lemon or lime juice, Worcestershire, Tabasco, salt, pepper and olive oil together.

- Top servings with balsamic vinegar and/or light sour cream.

Pam O'Malley

Susan's Lemony Basil Soup

1¼ cups onion, chopped
1 pound fresh mushrooms, sliced
1 cup carrots, sliced
1 cup celery, chopped
4 cloves garlic, minced
1/4 cup butter
6 cups water
1 49-ounce can chicken broth
1 10¾-ounce can cream of chicken soup
1/2 cup fresh basil, chopped
1 teaspoon lemon juice
1/2 cup wild rice, uncooked
1/4 cup regular rice, uncooked
Parmesan cheese, grated
Lemon slices

- In a 5-quart Dutch oven, sauté the onions, mushrooms, carrots, celery and garlic in butter until tender.

- Stir in water, chicken broth, cream of chicken soup, basil, lemon juice, wild rice and regular rice. Bring to a boil. Reduce heat. Cover and simmer 35 – 40 minutes.

- Garnish each serving with grated Parmesan cheese and a lemon slice.

Gail Selvala

Water

When a homesteader's cabin wasn't near a spring or brook, getting water was quite a chore. A large rain water tub or several rain barrels, tightly lidded, served in place of a well. In winter the barrels were filled with snow but in other seasons when fresh cool water was needed, one had to walk with a neck yoke hung with two buckets, to the nearest pond or stream.

Hand pumping water into cisterns was the norm in the early resort years before the arrival of electricity.

Laundry day at the McFarland cottage, 1937

Mary's Cold Curried Pea Soup

SERVES 8
2 Vidalia or other sweet onions, thinly sliced
3 tablespoons unsalted butter
2 tablespoons curry powder
4 cups low sodium chicken broth
2 cups peas, fresh preferred
2 tablespoons fresh mint leaves
Salt and cayenne pepper to taste
Plain yogurt

- Melt butter in a saucepan over medium heat and cook the onion until soft but not browned for approximately 20 minutes.

- Add curry powder and cook about 2 minutes.

- Add chicken broth and bring to a boil. Add peas and remove from heat.

- Cool then purée with mint leaves. Chill.

- Serve with a dollop of yogurt.

Jane Cardinal

Birch Bark Work

Indian Moccasins

Joe Ettawageshik
Indian Rustic Work Shop
Harbor Springs, Michigan
At the Ferry Dock

"Pommawanga"—The Indian Game

Post Cards

Souvenirs

Corn and Potato Chowder

1/2 pound bacon
1 onion, diced
2 14½-ounce cans creamed corn
1 can sliced potatoes
2 cups whole milk
Salt and pepper to taste

- Cook the bacon in a skillet. Cook the onion in a small amount of reserved bacon fat. Drain on paper towels.

- Add creamed corn, potatoes, milk, salt and pepper. Cook but do not boil.

- Add bacon just before serving.

Marge Edwards

The Old Trail Inn

Bob Edwards, his brother Jim, and Gene Moore bought The Old Trail Inn property in 1964 for $33,000. The property consisted of the Inn, four large cottages, five small housekeeping cottages on the bluff and a stretch of lakefront below.

In 1979, Bob and Marge Edwards built their home on the bluff where the "Squirrel's Nest" once stood. Jim and Mary Edwards built a cottage on the beach soon after. The group sold the remainder of the large cottages and the Moore family retained the Inn and the small cottages.

A Postcard View of The Old Trail Tavern, later Old Trail Inn

Schoolcraft Lodge

Aunt Agnes inherited the Schoolcraft from her sister Helen. It was of rustic design and sat on the bluff overlooking the lake just past The Old Trail Inn. Agnes was famous along the shore for her "storytelling days." She invited all children, summer residents and Lodge visitors to come (properly attired, of course) for tea and her beautifully read Uncle Remus stories. Before electricity and the diversion of radio, this was a special occasion. Older residents still recall it with pleasure. The Wortley family now proudly owns the Schoolcraft.

The Schoolcraft fireplace . . . the setting of Uncle Remus stories told by Aunt Agnes

Autumn Bisque

SERVES 4 to 6

1 (1 pound) butternut squash, peeled, cut in half, seeds removed
2 green apples, peeled, cored and chopped
1 medium onion, chopped
A pinch of rosemary
A pinch of marjoram
1 quart chicken stock or canned chicken broth
2 slices white bread, crusts trimmed and torn into pieces
1½ teaspoons salt, optional
1/2 teaspoon pepper
2 egg yolks
1/4 cup light cream

- Combine squash, apples, onion, herbs, stock, bread, salt and pepper in a heavy saucepan. Bring to a boil and simmer uncovered for 30 to 40 minutes.

- Purée the soup in a blender until smooth.

- Beat the egg yolks and cream together. Beat a small amount of the soup mixture into the egg and cream mixture. Gradually stir the egg, cream and soup mixture back into the saucepan of soup. Heat but do not boil.

The Wortley Family

Wild Rice, Chicken and Mushroom Soup

1 cup celery, chopped
1 cup fresh mushrooms, sliced
1 cup yellow onion, diced
1/4 cup butter
1/3 cup all-purpose flour
6 cups chicken stock
1 pound cooked chicken or turkey, skin removed and cubed
2 cups cooked wild rice
1 cup half and half
3 tablespoons sherry
2 tablespoons fresh lemon juice

- Sauté celery, mushrooms and onion in butter in a large saucepan until the celery is transparent. Reduce heat and blend in the flour, stirring to form a paste. Add the chicken stock and mix until smooth.

- Stir in chicken or turkey and cooked wild rice. Cook until the soup thickens.

- Remove from heat and stir in half and half, sherry and lemon juice. Heat thoroughly but do not boil.

Trina Hayes

The First Anti-Saloon League

The first anti-saloon league in the United States was established in Harbor Springs. Around 1827, a Catholic church made of cedar logs covered with bark was built by the Indians in Harbor Springs under the direction of Father Peter De Jean, the first resident priest. Father De Jean established a liquor law prohibiting the use and sale of liquor. The tribal chiefs strictly enforced the law that remained in place until 1854.

1910, the Indian warrior temperance maidens of Holy Childhood School

Healthy Kielbasa Vegetable Soup

SERVES 8 (MAKES 4 QUARTS)

My wife, Judith, spent summers in Cross Village, nearly all of her school years. We visited the area beginning in the early 1960s. Upon retirement in 2004, we became permanent Cross Village residents.

1/2 pound Smithfield hickory-smoked, NO MSG, kielbasa
3 large mushrooms (Any kind but portabellas are good.)
4 stalks organic celery, with tops
4 large carrots, organic
4 medium russet potatoes
1 medium onion
48 ounces (6 cups) water
1 14.5-ounce can Muir Glen fire-roasted, organic, crushed tomatoes
Olive oil for cooking the kielbasa
1 clove garlic, chopped
1/4 rounded tablespoon each of
Rosemary, Thyme, Summer Savory, Oregano
1/8 teaspoon black pepper
Parsley flakes
Do NOT add salt.

- Cut kielbasa, mushrooms and all vegetables into various sizes of chunks, slices and triangles. Chop the celery tops, but not fine as this shouldn't look like canned soup.

- Boil water in a large stainless steel pot (not Teflon). Add tomatoes and return to boil. Add the celery, carrots, potatoes and onion. Return to boil. Reduce to medium heat for 20 to 25 minutes.

- Meanwhile, put about 1/8-inch olive oil in a 12" stainless steel frying pan (no Teflon). When hot enough to make a drop of water sizzle, add the chunks of kielbasa, cooking thoroughly and browning all sides. Remove from heat.

- When vegetables are still firm but nearly done, stir in the kielbasa with the olive oil, mushrooms, garlic, and the first 4 herbs and pepper. Simmer until the vegetables are done but not mushy, about 5 minutes. Sprinkle parsley flakes to cover half the surface and stir in. It's done.

- This recipe can be doubled and freezes well.

John Knoppe

Joe Kishego dances at a homecoming festival

Mary Ellen Hughes

... from The Crow Bar to ...

The Crow's Nest

Andy and Sophie Wrona (Wrona is the word for crow in Polish) farmed the land around their little Cross Village home in the early 1950s. They owned 20 acres on State Road across from Beckon Road and also had a 10-acre apple orchard. Over time they opened a flat-roofed bar and added an eatery onto the front of their bungalow home.

Building the bar was easy compared to getting licensed for a six-burner, bottled gas stove. To encourage the beer-drinking regulars to think about food, Sophie sautéed onions in butter and offered hamburgers. Eventually the fresh, home-raised chicken dinner and a diverse array of homemade relishes served on Lazy Susans made the Crow Bar a local favorite. The Crow Bar also featured homemade apple and local berry pies and homemade soups.

In 1970, when Mary Ellen and Harmon Hughes bought the Crow Bar from the Wronas, in addition to the treasured relish recipe book, they also inherited a second family. Sophie's sister, Jenny Bodzick, remained as dishwasher and her daughter as a waitress. Her brother, Frank Wiklanski, did general maintenance, mowed the lawn, grew the produce in the garden and cut up the chickens. Andy Wrona's brother, Jack, ran the farm and sister Stella was the head waitress. Harmon had mastered all things culinary in the Navy so Mary Ellen tended the bar. She kept a mixing guide in hand and learned to turn off the spigot for patrons who didn't know their limits.

Mary Ellen and Harmon expanded the business, added space and soon the Crow Bar became The Crow's Nest. The following recipe is still a favorite at Mary Ellen's Place in Harbor Springs which she has owned since selling The Crow's Nest to Mike McElroy.

Harmon and Mary Ellen Hughes, 1979

A Celebrity Chef offering . . . Mary Ellen Hughes

Golumbki (Golabki)

This simple, hearty soup is just the ticket for a family coming in from a winter outing and it's not too demanding on the cook.

1 pound ground beef
1 large cabbage, chopped in large bite-sized squares
1 large Spanish onion, diced
1 tablespoon garlic, minced
1 tablespoon white pepper
1 tablespoon chicken base or use chicken broth but not
   bouillon cubes
1 tablespoon beef base or use beef broth but not
   bouillon cubes
1/2 cup long grain rice (not instant)
1 26-ounce can tomato soup

- Brown the ground beef; drain it and set it aside.
- Put the cabbage in a large pot along with the onion, garlic and pepper. Add water to fill the pot or adjust to accommodate if using canned liquid broth. Bring to a boil and add the ground beef then add the rice.
- In a separate bowl, whisk the tomato soup with some of the soup liquid to loosen, then add to the pot. Stir in the soup and heat until the rice is fully cooked.

Mary Ellen Hughes
Chef/Owner Mary Ellen's Place

The Crow's Nest as remodeled by the Hughes family

A Celebrity Chef offering . . . Val Wichtner

Cream of Mushroom Soup

Makes 8 to 10 bowls of soup
1 large onion, diced
Butter or margarine
1½ cups flour
3 quarts water or more (at least 12 cups), divided
1/2 quart Half & Half
1/2 quart heavy whipping cream
2 – 2½ pounds fresh mushrooms, sliced
1 carrot
Salt and pepper to taste

- Dice the onion and simmer in butter or margarine in a 6-quart kettle until soft.

- Mix flour and simmered onions together then slowly add at least 4 – 6 cups of water and mix until there are no lumps. Add more water if necessary.

- Mix 2 quarts water, 1/2 quart Half & Half and 1/2 quart heavy whipping cream together and stir into the onion and flour mixture. Fold in the fresh mushrooms.

- Grate the carrot; add to the mixture and stir well. Add salt and pepper to taste.

- Simmer for 90 minutes to 2 hours.

Val Harbus Wichtner

Val (right) and her daughters Kasha (left) and Tanya (center) ran the Village Café in Cross Village. It was a cherished local favorite famous for friendly down-home meals, oh-so-delicate pastries and Val's mushroom soup.

Easy Tuscan Soup

SERVES 4
2 tablespoons olive oil
1 cup carrots, sliced
1 cup onions, chopped
1/2 cup celery, chopped
2 garlic cloves, minced
1 can Great Northern beans, drained and rinsed
1 can black beans, drained and rinsed
1 14.5-ounce can chicken or vegetable broth
1/2 teaspoon dried thyme leaves
Salt and pepper to taste
Parmesan or Romano cheese, grated

- In a 5-quart Dutch oven, heat oil over medium-high heat until hot. Add carrots, onions, celery and garlic. Cook 4 to 5 minutes or until onions are tender, stirring occasionally.

- Stir in beans, broth and thyme. Bring to a boil. Reduce heat to medium. Simmer 10 minutes. Season to taste and serve with a sprinkling of cheese.

- Enjoy this soup with crusty Italian bread.

Sue Adams

Split Pea Soup

1 pound dried split peas, washed
48 ounces (6 cups) water
1 ham bone
1 carrot, grated
2 teaspoons salt
Black pepper, freshly ground, to taste

- Combine dried split peas, water, ham bone and grated carrot in a pot and simmer for 2 hours.
- Add salt and simmer an additional hour.
- Cut the ham off the bone, chop the ham and return it to the soup.
- Season with freshly ground pepper.

Sally Kelsey

Early Cross Village

Black Bean Soup

1 cup onion, diced
2 cloves garlic, minced
1¼ cups vegetable broth
2 15-ounce cans black beans, drained and rinsed
1 15-ounce can diced tomatoes
1 cup potatoes, diced
1/2 teaspoon dried thyme
1/2 teaspoon cumin
1/2 teaspoon Tabasco Sauce

- Combine and simmer.

Kira Stolen

The Chicago & West Michigan R.R., later the Pere Marquette rail line heading toward Harbor Springs

'Twas Labor Day Sunday,
And all thru Good Hart,
We eagerly waited
For the mini fair's start.

The Extension Club Gals
For months had been
   working:
No member escaped —
'Twas no time for shirking!

They'd sewed and they'd
   knitted
And pasted with glee;
Such labor was fun,
Mixed with cookies and tea!

As Sunday drew nigh,
All the ovens were busy,
Turning out goodies
At a pace that was dizzy.

There were coffeecakes,
   sweet rolls,
Zucchini bread too,
And donuts and muffins —
To name just a few.

There were jellies and jams,
Maple syrup as well.
The shelves would be _laden_
With goodies to sell.

The day finally dawned,
But no sun anywhere!
O no! It _can't_ rain!
It will _ruin_ the fair!

The firemen came first
And unloaded their trucks;
All the things they unloaded
Should bring in the bucks!

Then Myrt and her crew
Set to work fixing food.
Such a talent they have!
Everything tasted so good!

Continued next page

Mini Fair French Country Soup

SERVES 12

Make your own jar of French Country Soup mix or buy it at the RFC Mini Fair in July.

SOUP MIX:
1½ cups (12 ounces) assorted dried beans (Great Northern, lentils, green and yellow split peas, red kidney beans, baby limas, black-eyed peas, pinto beans, etc. or use a mixed bean package). Try to use at least 8 kinds of beans.

BOUQUET GARNI:
1 teaspoon parsley
3-4 peppercorns
1/8 teaspoon nutmeg
1/4 teaspoon celery seed
1/4 teaspoon thyme
1/4 teaspoon rosemary
2 small bay leaves
1/8 teaspoon cayenne
1/8 teaspoon garlic powder

- Mix beans together in a large bowl. Place 12-ounce portions in plastic bags.
- Cut a clean piece of cotton or muslin into a 3.5-inch square or use disposable tea filter bags (available at Primitive Images in Good Hart). Measure spices onto the fabric square or into the tea filter bag and tie with a piece of thread to close.
- To give as a gift, place the beans in a jar, top it with the "Bouquet Garni" bag and give a copy of the recipe below with the soup mix.

TO MAKE THE SOUP:

1 jar French Country Soup Mix including Bouquet Garni

3 quarts water

2 teaspoon salt

1 ham hock

2 cups onion, chopped

2 cups celery, chopped

1 green pepper, chopped

2 cloves garlic, minced

1 28-ounce can tomatoes, undrained

1 pound sliced smoked or turkey sausage (optional)

2 whole, raw, boneless, skinless chicken breasts, sliced in bite-sized pieces

- Rinse and drain beans. Place beans and spice bag from the jar of French Country Soup mix in a large covered stockpot. Add water, ham hock and salt and simmer at least 3 hours or until the beans are soft.

- Add onions, celery, green pepper, garlic and tomatoes to the stockpot with bean mixture.

- Simmer uncovered 90 minutes.

- Remove ham hock. Remove meat from bone and return chopped meat to pot.

- Add sausage and chicken and simmer 40 minutes.

- This soup can be made a day ahead or frozen.

Trina Hayes

A quilt fund-raiser pre Mini Fair Days. Betty Post, Ginny Thornberry, Marian Wines and Betty Glass.

We went merrily on,
And tried to ignore
A few rumblings of thunder,
'Tho we heard more and
more.

Some tarpaulins were hung,
To be safe — "just in case"—
For who wants to eat hot
dogs
With rain on their face?

Alas and alack,
It finally came!
The rain fell in <u>torrents</u>!
O <u>darn</u>! What a shame!

The cyclists came riding;
They were soaked to the
skin;
But their spirits were high;
They rode in with a grin.

They ate and they drank
And rested a while,
Then rode off again
With a satisfied smile.

And rain never stopped,
And some tarps began
leaking;
And the craft booth was
moved —
A dry spot they were
seeking.

But wonder of wonders,
The people kept coming!
They ate and they bought —
The cash boxes were
humming!

We finally closed shop;
It was well after four.
We were soggy and damp
And tired to the core.

But 'tho wet, we'd had fun,
And 'twas something to hear
All the plans being made
For the same time next
year!!

Sue Sutherland

Hungarian Goulash

1/4 pound bacon, diced
1 small onion, finely chopped
2 teaspoons vegetable oil
3 pounds stewing beef, cut in large cubes
3 tablespoon flour
1 teaspoon salt
1/4 teaspoon garlic powder
1 cup catsup
3 cups boiling water
5 medium potatoes, peeled and cut in large chunks. Place potatoes in a bowl and cover with water to prevent browning.

- Preheat oven to 325⁰.

- In a large Dutch oven or stock pot, cook bacon and onions over medium heat until the onions are soft. Do not brown the onions or bacon. Remove from pot and set aside.

- Add vegetable oil to pan as needed and brown meat in 3 batches.

- Put all meat, bacon and onions back into the pot. Sprinkle flour over meat and stir.

- Add remaining ingredients except potatoes.

- Bring mixture to a simmer over medium heat, stirring until sauce begins to thicken.

- Cover the pot and put it in the preheated 325⁰ oven for 2 hours.

- Drain the potatoes and add to the pot. Bake an additional 1 – 2 hours until the potatoes are soft.

Linda Little

South African Lamb Stew

1 cup dried apples
1/2 cup dried, pitted prunes
1/2 cup seedless raisins
1½ cups water
1½ pounds boneless lamb shoulder (or beef chuck), cubed
1 teaspoon salt
2 tablespoons vegetable oil
1 cup onion, finely chopped
2 tablespoons curry powder
2 tablespoons red wine vinegar
1 tablespoon lemon juice
1/4 cup salted peanuts, chopped
2 medium bananas, sliced 1/8" thick, just before serving

- Combine apples, prunes, raisins and water. Soak at least 1 hour, turning frequently.

- Salt meat and brown in oil. Transfer to a plate. Pour off all but 2 tablespoons of oil and cook the onions in it until soft.

- Reduce heat and add curry powder. Cook another 2 minutes.

- Return meat to the skillet along with fruits and their liquid, vinegar and lemon juice. Bring to a boil and reduce heat.

- Simmer covered for 1 hour or until the meat is tender if using lamb. (If using beef, simmer 2½ to 3 hours.) Stir occasionally and add up to 1/4 cup water if needed.

- To serve, mound the meat on a platter, sprinkle with chopped peanuts and arrange the slices of banana around the meat. Serve over rice.

Jane Cardinal

The Hiawatha Pageant, 1905 – 1917

The dramatic outdoor presentation of The Song of Hiawatha drew throngs of tourists to Round Lake (just outside Petoskey near Bay View). The Grand Rapids and Indiana Railroad sponsored the event that featured Native American actors. Ella Petoskey, granddaughter of Chief Ignatius Petoskey, played Minnehaha. This postcard showing Ella Petoskey was so popular that it made northern Michigan a brief point of notice on the world stage.

Feijoada (fay-o-ah-da)

This is a make-ahead Argentinean stew, hearty and filling and perfect for a cold night. It's also a meat lover's dream!

1 pound dried black beans, plus cold water for soaking
2 tablespoons vegetable oil
1 pound boneless ham, cut in cubes
1 pound boneless pork loin, cubed
3/4 pound hot (or fennel) Italian sausage, cut into chunks
3/4 pound smoked sausage, sliced
1½ cups tomato purée
1/2 to 1 cup chicken broth
1 pint cherry tomatoes, left whole or cut in half
1 large onion, coarsely chopped
6 cloves garlic, chopped
1 teaspoon red pepper flakes
1/8 teaspoon orange zest
6 cups water, approximately
Cilantro to taste

The cut made by the washout at Talbot Beach

- Cover beans with cold water and soak overnight. Drain. (If in a hurry, cover beans with boiling water, let stand for 2 hours and drain.)
- Preheat oven to 350⁰.
- Brown meat in batches in oil. Drain fat.
- In a large Dutch oven, combine the browned meat with the remaining ingredients except cilantro, add 6 cups of water and bring to a boil. Remove from the heat and skim the fat.
- Cover and transfer to a preheated 350⁰ oven and bake for 90 minutes. Remove cover and bake for another 30 minutes, stirring occasionally.
- Allow to cool, cover and refrigerate overnight allowing the flavors to blend.
- Before reheating, remove any fat from the surface. Reheat slowly to serve.
- Serve over white rice with a garnish of cilantro

Carolyn Shear

It was Heard Miles Away

The weather took a freaky twist as spring began in 1924. Three feet of snow lay on the ground when a hot spell caused a quick melt. Sand bags were laid along State Road to direct the gushing water toward the bay in order to save the hill road into Harbor Springs. But north of Good Hart, with one mighty roar, a few miles of land slipped lakeward down a streambed. One of the best "resort" beaches, the Talbot, was forever altered. Today, when passing that area of water by boat, you can see the jumble of trees that were driven into the lake that day.

1924, the road and culvert replacement

Legs Inn

Founder Stanley Smolak knew how important the tavern his family owned and ran in Poland was to binding a community. The Smolak family musicians kept things lively at the tavern and Stan's father also taught his son to build furniture as he had.

Beginning in the 1920s when he arrived in Cross Village, Stanley spent much of his time in the forests and along the shoreline collecting stones, twisted roots, mammoth burls, knots and driftwood that soon became his medium for the furniture, fixtures and sculptures that make up Legs Inn. The bar was sculpted from a hemlock tree and decorated with local fieldstone. Stanley used a row of inverted stove legs to decorate the railing of the roof surrounding the building, thus giving Legs Inn its name.

Legs Inn opened in the 1920s and has welcomed visitors ever since. Polish dinners were featured then and continue to-

Continued next page

Bigos – Traditional Polish Hunter's Stew

A traditional Polish stew is said to have been introduced by Wladislaus II, a prince who became King in 1385 and who supposedly served it to his hunting party guests. Bigos recipes vary widely. This is our favorite.

8 slices bacon
1/2 pound boneless lean pork shoulder or venison
1/2 pound lean beef, cubed
1 onion, sliced
2 carrots, sliced or cubed
1/2 – 1 pound sliced mushrooms
2 bay leaves
2 cups beef stock
1 16-ounce can or 2 cups sauerkraut, rinsed and drained well
4 cups cabbage, shredded
1 6-ounce can or 4 tablespoons tomato paste
5 dried prunes or 1/4 cup dry red wine
1/4 teaspoon salt
1/8 teaspoon pepper
1/2 – 1 pound kielbasa smoked sausage, coarsely sliced

Jan and Stan Smolak

George and Kathy Smolak

- Fry the bacon in a Dutch oven or large saucepan over high heat for 3 minutes. Drain off some of the fat leaving just enough to coat the pot. Add the beef and pork or venison and the onion, carrots and mushrooms. Stirring constantly, cook until the meat is browned on all sides for about 5 minutes.

- Reduce heat to medium; add the bay leaves, beef stock, rinsed and drained sauerkraut, cabbage, tomato paste, dried prunes or wine and spices. Bring to a boil increasing heat level if necessary. Reduce heat, cover and simmer for 1 hour, stirring occasionally to prevent sticking.

- Add the kielbasa and stir. Cover and simmer over low heat for 30 minutes. The flavor intensifies when reheated the next day.

SMACZNEGO!
Kathy and George Smolak
Owners, Legs Inn

day. Stan's wife Elizabeth was known for her fine gardens where she grew the produce to feed the patrons of the hotel they had on the bluff until the tavern opened. Today an outdoor garden area is filled with lavish perennial beds and a Lake Michigan view.

Current owners George Smolak (Stanley's nephew), his wife Kathy and their sons Mark and Chris employ over 40 people during the peak season including students from Poland who bring their culture to the delight of tourists and local residents. They offer entertainment during the summer and are famous for their unusual imported Polish beers and vodkas.

In a competition of over 40,000 entries, Travelocity cited Legs Inn as one of the Top Ten local secrets and big finds in Michigan.

Firehouse Chili

3 pounds lean ground sirloin
1 pound pork tenderloin, cubed
2 links Italian sausage
Salt to taste
2 large onions, chopped
3 cloves garlic, chopped
2 tablespoons chili powder
2 tablespoons ground cumin
1 tablespoon dried oregano
2 tablespoons all-purpose flour
1 cup tomato sauce
6 ounces tomato paste
2 pounds tomatoes, chopped
2 stalks celery, chopped
1 medium green bell pepper, chopped
2 bay leaves
1 tablespoon brown sugar
2 tablespoons freshly squeezed lemon juice
3 15-ounce cans pinto beans, drained and rinsed
1 16-ounce can red kidney beans, drained and rinsed
1 4½-ounce can mild jalapeno peppers, chopped
1 cup red wine
Sour cream and lime wedges, for garnish
Warmed flour tortillas, as an accompaniment

The RFC, 2011

- In a large skillet, brown the sirloin, pork and sausage. Drain all but 2 tablespoons of fat and transfer meat to a large stockpot. Salt to taste and keep warm over low heat.

- In the same skillet, sauté the onions and garlic until tender. Add to the meat and mix thoroughly.

- In a small bowl, combine the chili powder, cumin, oregano and flour. Sprinkle over the meat and stir to coat well.

- Stir in the tomato sauce, tomato paste and tomatoes and increase the heat to medium. Add water if mixture seems too dry.

- Add celery, green pepper, bay leaves, brown sugar and lemon juice. Simmer, covered for 2 hours or more, stirring occasionally. During the last 40 minutes, add pinto beans, red kidney beans, jalapeno peppers and wine.

- Garnish bowls of chili with sour cream and lime wedges. Serve with warm flour tortillas.

Lindsey Pfaff
Former RFC First Responder

Baked Chili

Jo Henderson shared this recipe with our family many years ago. The Hendersons were long-time Good Hart residents.

1½ pounds ground beef
1 cup onions, chopped
1 cup celery, chopped
2 cloves garlic, chopped
1 can condensed tomato soup
2 cans kidney beans, drained and rinsed
2 tablespoons (or more to taste) chili powder

- Preheat the oven to 225°.
- Cook the ground beef until crumbly but not browned. Transfer the ground beef to a 2-quart casserole.
- In the same skillet used to cook the ground beef, sauté the onions, celery and garlic but do not brown.
- Add the tomato soup, kidney beans and chili powder then add the mixture to the beef in the casserole. Stir together. Bake covered for 2½ hours in the preheated 225° oven.

Ken Kelsey
RFC First Responder and
Fire Board Member

White Chicken Chili

SERVES 8 to 10

This tastes even better on the second day and freezes well. Adjust the spices, chicken and cheese to your liking.

1 pound Great Northern beans, soaked overnight in water and drained
6 cups (+) chicken broth or stock
3 cloves garlic, minced
2 medium onions, chopped and divided
1 tablespoon olive oil
1 4-ounce can chopped green chilies (Use 2 cans for more heat.)
1 tablespoon ground cumin
2 teaspoons oregano
1/4 teaspoon cayenne pepper or more to taste
1/4 teaspoon ground cloves
3 cups or more diced, cooked chicken breast meat
2 cups or more grated Monterey Jack cheese
(You may use Pepper Jack cheese for extra kick.)

- Combine beans, chicken broth, garlic and half the onions in a soup pot and bring to a boil over high heat. Reduce heat to low and simmer until beans are soft (2 – 3 hours). Add more chicken broth if necessary to maintain desired consistency.

- In a skillet, sauté the remaining onions in olive oil over medium-high heat until tender, about 5 minutes. Add chilies (1 or 2 cans depending on how spicy you want it), cumin, oregano, cayenne pepper and cloves. Mix thoroughly then add to the bean mixture.

- Add chicken and simmer 1 hour or more to blend flavors. Stir in cheese and allow to melt completely just before serving.

Trina Hayes

An Indian trail, 1930s

141

Recipe For:_____

_____
_____
_____
_____
_____
_____
_____
_____
_____
_____
_____
_____
_____
_____
_____
_____
_____
_____
_____
_____
_____
_____
_____
_____
_____
_____
_____
_____
_____
_____
_____
_____
_____
_____
_____

Main Dishes

Panoramic View from Lake Shore Drive, 1950s, by Virgil D. Haynes
©Haynes Studio, Harbor Springs

Recipes

A Heritage Recipe . . .

Christina's Baked Steak

My mother, Christina Sims, used to make this baked steak on our wood-burning kitchen stove in "The Shadows," our cottage built in 1938 on "the low road," now Lamkin Road. It is a favorite family recipe even now with an electric stove.

3 pounds beef round steak, approximately
1 or 2 onions, sliced
Butter or bacon fat
Flour
Salt
Pepper
1-2 cups boiling water

- Brown the sliced onions in a pan with butter or bacon fat. (This can be done the previous day.)
- Preheat the oven to 300^0.
- While browning the onions, pound flour, salt and pepper into both sides of the steak with the edge of a saucer.
- Place the steak in the pan and cook until browned on both sides.
- Boil approximately 1 cup water.
- Place the pan containing the steak and onions in the preheated 300^0 oven and carefully pour the boiling water into the pan just to cover the steak.
- Cook 1 to 2 hours. Add water when needed.
- Turn off the oven and leave in the oven overnight.
- The following day, heat the oven to 250^0 and cook for 2 to 3 hours, keeping covered with boiling water for gravy.

Sue Schulze

The Old Convent in Cross Village was built by The Benevolent Charitable and Religious Society of Saint Francis under the direction of Fr. John Bernard Weikamp. The convent of 200 nuns and brothers managed 2,000 wooded and farmed acres regarded for exemplary harvests.

On one of the postcards of this early photo Father Weikamp wrote the following under the picture: "Everyone who enters, or being in this church during Public Services have to avoid all disorder and comply into the external ceremonies as kneeling seating and standing up; and everyone who is not willing to comply with this rule does better to stay away, as to give scandal! And has to expect to be shown or put out of doors."

Perfect Roast Beef

I obtained this recipe from Chef Louis Szathmary of the famed Chicago Bakery. It always results in a perfect roast that is a family favorite.

1 7 – 8 pound U.S. Choice 4 rib or standing rib roast
4 tablespoons Kitchen Bouquet
4 tablespoons corn oil
1 small garlic clove
1 cup chef's salt (see recipe below)
1 carrot, scraped and coarsely chopped
1 large onion, unpeeled and coarsely chopped
4 – 6 tablespoons shortening, optional

CHEF'S SALT:
1 cup salt
1 tablespoon Spanish paprika
1 teaspoon ground black pepper
1/4 teaspoon ground white pepper
1/4 teaspoon celery salt
1/4 teaspoon garlic salt (don't use garlic powder)

- Preheat oven to 375⁰.

- Mix Kitchen Bouquet and corn oil and rub the entire surface of the roast especially the two cut ends and the surface of the bony part with the mixture.

- Score the fat on top if desired.

CROSS VILLAGE CONVENT, CROSS VILLAGE MICH.

- Crush the garlic to a pulp with some of the chef's salt. Rub the entire amount of the chef's salt and garlic mixture into the surface of the roast, including the fat, covering completely. Note: the meat won't be salty nor will the salt draw out the juices.

- Pour water 1 inch deep in the bottom of a roasting pan and add the coarsely chopped carrot and onion.

- Place the roast on top of the vegetables, fat side up.

- Roast the meat in the preheated 375^0 oven, uncovered, for 30 minutes.

- Cover the pan and continue roasting until a meat thermometer registers the desired temperature: 100^0 for rare, 115^0 for medium rare, or 140^0 for medium.

- Remove the roast from the oven and let it rest on a board for at least 60 minutes.

- 10 minutes before serving, set the oven temperature as high as possible. Put the roast on a cookie sheet or jelly roll pan and place in the oven for 10 minutes.

- If you prefer a dark, crusty surface, heat 4 – 6 tablespoons of shortening until smoking and pour the hot fat over the beef before returning it to the oven.

Jane Cardinal

The reverse of the postcard on the opposite page. This card was written in Odawa by a Native American resident of Cross Village in 1910. At that time Cross Village was still principally an Indian village.

Best Beef Brisket

I like to fix this when entertaining eight to ten people for dinner. It can be prepared a day or two ahead and marinated in the sauce until ready to bake.

2¼ cups catsup
1½ cups beer
1/2 cup packed brown sugar
1/2 cup white wine vinegar
2 tablespoons Worcestershire Sauce
2 tablespoons chili powder
3 garlic cloves, minced
1 cup onion, chopped
1/4 teaspoon cayenne pepper
1 5 – 7 pound beef brisket, trimmed of excess fat
2 tablespoons liquid smoke

- Combine catsup, beer, brown sugar, white wine vinegar, Worcestershire Sauce, chili powder, garlic, onion and cayenne pepper in a large sauce pan. Bring to a boil; reduce heat and simmer. Stir occasionally and cook until the sauce thickens.

- Pour 2 cups of the sauce in a bowl and refrigerate.

- Preheat oven to 250⁰.

- Rub liquid smoke over each side of the brisket.

- Brush both sides of the brisket with some of the sauce and place in a large baking dish. Pour the remaining sauce over the brisket and turn over, cover and bake for 4 hours or until tender.

- Remove the brisket from the pan juices and slice thinly across the grain.

- Heat the reserved liquid and serve over the sliced brisket.

Connie Cobb

Marinade for Grilled Flank Steak

1 flank steak, about 2 pounds to serve 4 – 6

MARINADE:
1/4 cup oil
1/4 cup soy sauce
2 tablespoons lemon juice
2 garlic cloves
1/2 teaspoon celery salt
6 green onions, chopped with the tops

- Mix marinade ingredients and marinate the flank steak for at least 3 hours.
- Grill to taste.
- Serve with potatoes sliced with onion, salt, butter, pepper, rosemary and a little vegetable oil wrapped in foil and placed on the grill about 25 minutes before grilling the meat.

Carolyn Shear

In the early days of summer cottages, most were without running water. Rural Electrification didn't come until the 40s. Going to the Good Hart Store was a daily trek. Cliff Powers would cut a side of beef from one end to the other. You got what came up. The cleaver would come down smartly on the immense stump that was his butcher block. Bones were sawn and your meat was wrapped in butcher paper and tied with the string that hung from a dispensing spool that hung above the counter.

Cliff Powers calculating a tab on his adding machine

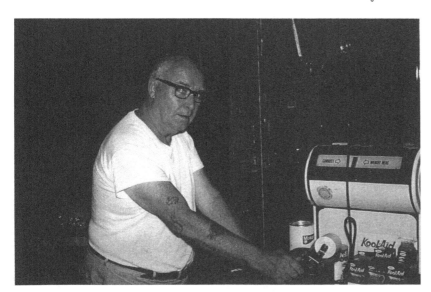

Moroccan Pot Roast

This is a summertime favorite at our cottage. It's tender, feeds a crowd and has a wonderful combination of flavors. It can also be prepared in a large pot on the stove if you don't want to use the oven. It's easy to put together and leaves time for entertaining. Serve it with a salad and some bread to sop up the flavorful broth.

1½ tablespoons olive oil
2 chuck roasts, 2– 3 pounds each
1 – 2 teaspoons sea salt
1 – 2 teaspoons freshly ground pepper
2 yellow onions, chopped
6 carrots (approximately 1 pound) cut into chunks
2 – 3 garlic cloves, chopped
2 tablespoons ground paprika
2 teaspoons ground cumin
2 teaspoons ground cinnamon
1 – 2 32-ounce boxes of low sodium beef broth
1 – 2 15-ounce cans chickpeas, rinsed and drained
1/2 cup dried apricots, chopped
1/2 cup golden raisins
1/4 to 1/2 cup fresh cilantro
1/4 cup fresh mint

- Preheat oven to 325⁰.
- Heat olive oil in a large, heavy duty roasting pan set over 2 burners on medium heat.

- Sprinkle each roast with sea salt and pepper. Sear roasts in the pan for 4 minutes on each side. Remove from pan and place on a platter.

- Add onion, carrot and garlic to the pan and cook stirring constantly for about 3 minutes. Add paprika, cumin and cinnamon to the vegetables and cook stirring constantly for 2 more minutes.

- Add broth and return the roasts to the roasting pan. Cover with aluminum foil and bake for 3 to 3½ hours or until fork tender.

- Remove the beef from the roasting pan and place on a platter. Tent with aluminum foil to keep warm.

- Skim the fat from the surface of the cooking liquid. Add the chickpeas to the liquid and heat. Stir in the remaining ingredients.

- Separate the meat into portions and spoon vegetables and liquid over the beef. Serve warm.

Janice Collins

CARDINAL
II

Marinade for Grilled Pot Roast

5 ounces soy sauce
1/4 cup brown sugar
1 tablespoon lemon juice
1/4 cup bourbon or blended whiskey (optional)
1½ cup water
1 teaspoon Worcestershire Sauce

- Combine all ingredients in a saucepan over low heat until brown sugar dissolves.
- Cover a thick cut of chuck roast, arm roast or round steak (2 – 3 inches) with the marinade and place in the refrigerator for 6 to 48 hours. Turn to cover all meat surfaces.

Sara Latimer
A Little-Latimer tradition

Mort Neff, Mr. Michigan Outdoors, kept a cottage in the environs of Good Hart. Here he is pictured with his tamed grouse named "Gussie."

Peanut Sauce for Chicken, Beef or Shrimp

This is delicious when served over grilled chicken, beef or shrimp and rice. I'm not sure how long it will keep in the refrigerator as my family eats it up so quickly.

1 cup creamy peanut butter (not old fashioned or freshly ground)
1 14-ounce can chicken broth
1/4 cup fresh lime juice
3 tablespoons brown sugar
2 tablespoons plus 1 teaspoon soy sauce
2 tablespoons chopped and peeled fresh ginger
1/2 teaspoon red pepper flakes
Chicken, beef or shrimp, grilled
Cooked rice

- Put peanut butter in a heavy sauce pan over gentle heat; gradually stir in chicken broth.

- Add the remaining ingredients and stir over medium heat until thickened and smooth for about 6 minutes.

- This can be made ahead and kept refrigerated for several days.

- If refrigerated, reheat and thin with more broth or water if necessary.

- Serve over rice with your choice of chicken, beef, shrimp or whatever you prefer.

Susan Carson

Golabki (Gowompki)

My mother, Jennie Lasley, made this often without using a recipe. You may have to make adjustments to the amounts for this delicious golabki. It's great for picnics.

1 large head of cabbage
1¼ pounds ground beef
4 cups cooked long grain rice
1 medium onion, diced
1 stick butter
1 can tomato soup
1 can cream of mushroom soup
Salt and pepper to taste
Oil

- Preheat oven to 350^0.
- Cut the cabbage core and soak the cabbage in boiling water until the leaves are limp. Peel off heavy ribs with paring knife.
- Mix the uncooked ground beef with the cooked rice. Salt and pepper and set aside.
- Sauté the diced onion in a stick of melted butter. Add soups and simmer for 10 minutes.
- Put cabbage leaf, rib side down; spoon meat and rice mixture into cabbage. Fold up, fold in the sides and fold the top down.
- Place in an oiled pan in layers.
- Pour sauce over to completely cover.
- Bake in a preheated 350^0 oven for 2 hours.

Deborah Root

Stuffed Cabbage

1 large head of cabbage
1 pound ground beef
2 eggs
1/2 cup raw rice
1 teaspoon salt
1/4 teaspoon pepper
1 onion, diced

SAUCE:
1 large onion, chopped
2 cups tomato sauce
2 1-pound cans tomatoes
2 tablespoons lemon juice
1/4 teaspoon pepper
1 teaspoon salt
1 teaspoon Worcestershire Sauce
3/4 cup brown sugar

- Preheat oven to 375°.
- Simmer cabbage to soften the leaves. Peel off the leaves and place on counter. Cut off the tough ribs.
- Combine ground beef, eggs, rice, salt, pepper and diced onion. Divide the mixture onto the leaves (about 12 – 15 sections). Roll up each section and tuck in the sides after the first turn.
- Chop the remaining cabbage and place it in the bottom of a large rectangular pan. Place the cabbage rolls onto the chopped cabbage, seam side down.
- Mix the sauce ingredients together and pour over the cabbage rolls.
- Bake covered in a preheated 375° oven for 1 hour. Reduce the oven temperature to 250° and bake uncovered for an additional 2 hours.

Anne Munger

Cross Village Days

We started building our cabin in Cross Village in 1964. Several young families with children had purchased old Indian homes or had built small cabins in the village. The children roamed freely and ate lunch wherever they were at lunchtime.

On Friday nights, when the husbands arrived for the weekend, the adults met at Legs Inn which was then a jukebox bar. The Veling girls watched the younger children. We danced to the jukebox until owner Stan Smolak decided it was time to close — usually around 10:30 or 11 p.m.

On Saturday nights we usually had pot luck at someone's home or at the old township hall where Nellie Pinterelli often brought her famous stuffed cabbage. After supper we often went to Harry Pinterelli's gas station to watch old reel movies or more often a travelogue of his trip to Alaska. The gas station was the heart of Cross Village. Most of us had no wells so our water was hauled in five gallon jerry cans from Harry's. We had elaborately decorated or painted outhouses in our yards. Life was uncomplicated and simple. I miss it (except the outhouse).

Good Soup, 1881

The basis for all good soups is the juice of the meat. This may be made by boiling the cracked joints of uncooked beef, veal or mutton; to these may be added the cracked bones of cooked game or underdone beef or mutton, but for the juices and nourishment, depend on the juice of uncooked meat, the rest being added for flavoring." (After the stock is skimmed and cooled, the other ingredients are added.)

Swedish Meatballs

SERVES 12

My grandfather was from the Arctic Circle in Sweden. We still have a smorgasbord every Christmas Eve. Even though it is smaller than in past years, we still look forward to the smells and traditions passed on through my mother. Having visited Sweden, northern Michigan reminds me of Scandinavia — trees with lots of water!

1 pound lean ground beef
1/2 to 1 pound ground pork
1/2 pound ground veal (Ask the butcher to grind the
      meat 2 – 3 times.)
1/2 cup bread crumbs
1 cup milk
1 egg, beaten
3 tablespoons chopped onion
1/4 teaspoon white pepper
1 teaspoon salt
Dash nutmeg
Dash allspice
2 tablespoons butter
2 14-ounce cans beef broth
Lingonberries, optional for serving

- Mix beef, pork, veal, bread crumbs, milk, egg, onion and spices together.
- Roll into balls smaller than for regular meatballs.
- Brown in 2 tablespoons of butter.
- Turn and shake the pan as meatballs brown.
- When meatballs are completely browned on all sides, add beef broth to pan and finish cooking over low heat until done.
- Suggestion: Serve with lingonberries on the side.

Kathy Bowers

German Applesauce Meatloaf

Many years ago I heard this recipe read on National Public Radio. It's a large recipe but it makes wonderful meatloaf sandwiches.

1½ pounds ground beef
1/2 pound ground pork
1 cup applesauce
1/2 cup or more diced onion
1 cup dry bread crumbs
1 egg
1 tablespoon salt
1 teaspoon pepper
1 tablespoon catsup

- Preheat oven to 350^0.
- Mix ground beef, ground pork, applesauce, diced onion, bread crumbs, egg, salt and pepper and place in an 8½" x 4½" bread pan or similar loaf pan.
- Spread the catsup over the top of the loaf.
- Bake in the oven for 2 hours.

Ed Stolt

A panorama of Harbor Springs when steamers brought summer visitors from Chicago and beyond – note the lumber docks at the right.

HARBOR SPRINGS, MICH.

1955, Gordie and Don Kruskie outside the family farmhouse

Top-of-the-Stove Meatloaf

My husband, Gordon, was born and raised in the farm house where we live on Island View Road. He attended schools in Cross Village and graduated from high school in Harbor Springs.

2 pounds ground round
1 pound ground pork sausage
1 egg
1 onion, chopped
4 slices cracked wheat bread
Enough milk to wet the bread
2½ teaspoons salt
Dash of pepper
Enough oatmeal to hold the loaf together
1/2 cup water

- Mix all ingredients except water and shape into 2 loaves.
- Using a frying pan with a high cover, cook the loaves on medium heat until browned on all sides (about 30 minutes).
- Turn heat down to simmer; add 1/2 cup water; cover and cook for 1 hour. Turn the loaves after 30 minutes.

Edith Kruskie

Santa Clara Pie

I made this quite often in the little log cabin we rented from Rhoda Herron when our kids were very young. They loved it and it was easy to cook in the small cabin kitchen. I bake these ahead so I'm prepared for company or a night when we feel like comfort food without the work. I keep one in the freezer to take whenever someone is in need of a meal.

2 deep dish pie crusts (Make your own or use frozen crusts.)
1 pound plus a little more lean ground beef, organic if possible
1 onion, chopped
1 green pepper, chopped
1 cup grated Monterey Jack cheese
1 16-ounce can stewed tomatoes
1 15-ounce can corn, drained or equivalent frozen corn, defrosted
1 15-ounce can kidney or black beans, rinsed and drained
2 teaspoons chili powder
1/2 teaspoon oregano
1/4 teaspoon pepper
1/2 teaspoon salt, if desired
1 cup crushed corn chips (plain Tostitos work well)

- Preheat oven to 425^0.
- Brown the beef, onion and pepper and drain well.
- Add half of the cheese to the pan and then add the stewed tomatoes with juice, corn, beans and spices.
- Cover and simmer for 5 minutes.
- Pour into pie crusts. (If using frozen crusts do not cook previously.)
- Top with the rest of the cheese and crushed chips.
- Bake in a preheated 425^0 oven for 20 minutes or according to pie crust recipe, until golden brown.

Trina Hayes

This makes two pies. Wrap one in plastic wrap when cool and freeze to use later.

If planning to freeze the pie, do not add the crushed chips until you reheat the pie.

To serve a frozen pie, defrost in the refrigerator and bake in a preheated 350^0 oven for about 20 minutes or until hot.

Hamburger Pot Pie with Onion Pastry

Even though I'm considered a good cook, I've never made this recipe. This Pot Pie is a favorite of my mother's, so if it is to be cooked, she shall do it. Currently 100-years young, she makes it quite often. You can tell it's an old recipe as it includes Crisco as an ingredient. When she first made this, it used lard.

PIE CRUST:
2 cups sifted all-purpose flour
3/4 cup Crisco
1 teaspoon onion salt
1/4 cup water

- Preheat oven to 400^0. If using a metal pie plate, preheat to 450^0.
- Sift the flour before measuring and spoon lightly into nested 1-cup measuring cup and level without shaking down.
- Cut Crisco into the flour with a pastry blender or 2 knives until the mixture is uniform.
- Mix onion salt and water; sprinkle water a tablespoon at a time over flour mixture; toss lightly with a fork. Work the dough into a firm ball with your hands.
- Divide in half and form 2 circles. On a lightly floured surface, roll out the bottom crust until 1½ inch larger than an inverted 9" pie plate. Cut a circle 1 inch larger than the inverted pie plate. Trim even with edge.
- Roll out the top crust the same way.
- Place pie crust in pie pan and fill with hamburger pie filling (recipe below) and cover with the top crust. Trim ½ inch beyond edge. Fold the top crust under the edge of the bottom crust; seal and flute with fingers or fork. Cut slits in top crust.
- Bake in preheated 400^0 oven (450^0 if using a metal pie pan) for 25 minutes.

HAMBURGER PIE FILLING:
1 tablespoon Crisco
1 pound lean ground beef
1/2 cup chopped onion
1 15-ounce can green beans, drained or 2 cups fresh or
    frozen green beans
1 10-ounce can tomato soup
1 teaspoon salt
1 tablespoon sugar
1/4 teaspoon pepper
1/8 teaspoon oregano

- Heat 1 tablespoon Crisco in a skillet. Add the ground beef and onion; cook just until the meat browns.
- Stir in green beans, soup and seasonings.
- Pour filling into onion pastry-lined pie plate, cover with top crust and bake as directed above.

Bob Smith
RFC Fire Board Member and
"Retired" Medical First Responder

Hacienda Hamburger

This is our "family's coming up tonight" dinner. I cook it early in the day, leave it at the back of the stove and warm it up when they arrive. I also put it in a casserole dish and take it to potlucks. The recipe came from a 1957 Grosse Pointe Memorial Church Cookbook.

1 pound ground beef
2 tablespoons vegetable or olive oil
3/4 cup chopped onion
1 cup celery, chopped
2½ cups canned tomatoes
3/4 cup ripe olives, sliced (If young children don't like ripe olives, use green.)
1½ teaspoons salt
1/4 teaspoon black pepper
2 cups uncooked wide noodles
A few drops Tabasco Sauce, optional
1/4 pound (American) cheddar cheese, diced
Tomato juice, if needed

- Brown ground beef in oil about 5 minutes, stirring frequently.
- Stir in the chopped onion and celery and cook about 5 additional minutes.
- Add tomatoes, olives, salt, pepper, uncooked noodles and Tabasco Sauce if desired. Cover and cook slowly for about 15 minutes.
- Stir in cheese and cook until the noodles are done.
- If it's too dry add a little tomato juice to moisten.

Mary Beth Mellen

Seven Layer Casserole

Use as much or as little of each ingredient as you desire.
Potatoes, sliced
Carrots, sliced
Celery, sliced
Onions, sliced
Rice, uncooked
Ground beef
Tomato juice

- Preheat oven to 350^0.
- Grease a 1½-quart casserole.
- Put a layer of sliced potatoes on the bottom of the casserole dish.
- Place a layer of sliced carrots over potatoes, then a layer of sliced celery and then a layer of sliced onion.
- Top with 1 tablespoon of uncooked rice.
- Brown the ground beef until no longer red. Drain.
- Place browned ground beef on top of casserole.
- Pour tomato juice over the top and bake in the preheated 350^0 oven until the carrots are tender.
- Season with salt and pepper to taste.

Marti Wallen

Photo by Cliff Powers

Cabbage Roll Casserole

2 pounds ground beef
1 cup chopped onion
1 29-ounce can tomato sauce
3½ pounds chopped cabbage
1 cup uncooked white rice
1 teaspoon salt
2 14-ounce cans beef broth

- Preheat oven to 350⁰.
- In a large skillet, brown the ground beef. Drain off the fat.
- In a large mixing bowl, combine onion, tomato sauce, cabbage, rice and salt.
- Add browned meat and mix together.
- Pour mixture into two 9" x 13" baking dishes.
- Pour 1 can of beef broth over each pan of meat mixture.
- Bake covered for 1 hour. Stir, replace cover and bake another 15 minutes.

Donna Wood

Campfire Foil Dinner

This is a huge favorite with our family. We love campfires on the beach, foil dinners, sunsets, scary stories and lots of laughter.

Cooking oil
Potatoes, sliced
Ground beef or chicken breast
Carrots, sliced
Onions, sliced
Seasoned salt
Ground pepper
Water

- Cut 2 squares of aluminum foil and place on top of each other, crimping the edges a bit.
- Spread 2 – 3 tablespoons of oil on the foil.
- Layer potato slices, meat, carrots and onion slices.
- Season to taste and sprinkle with water.
- Fold and seal into a foil packet.
- Cook over medium coals for 45 – 60 minutes.
- Open and enjoy.

Debbie Dicken

The McFarlands enjoy the beach at Good Hart, 1936.

Good Hart Campfire Dinner Beans

We live in a 100+ year old log cabin south of Good Hart and we love it. An 80-foot pine tree fell and just missed the cabin. My husband made a large picnic table with the stumps for legs and with plywood and a table cloth for the top. People love the look and the story. We love sharing our beautiful area with family and friends who visit over the campfire and the handmade table.

2 pounds ground beef
1 large onion, chopped
1 can kidney beans, undrained
1 can Great Northern Beans, drained
1 can lima beans, drained
1 can chili beans, undrained
1 can wax beans, drained
1 can tomato soup
1 cup brown sugar
2 celery ribs, chopped
2 teaspoons ground dry mustard

- Preheat oven to 350^0.
- Brown the ground beef and chopped onion until done. Drain and add the remaining ingredients and bring to a boil.
- Bake for 90 minutes. You can also cook this in a cast iron pot or skillet outside over a campfire.
- I generally cook it inside then bring it out to serve over the side of the campfire for fun and to keep it warm.

Kathy Bowers

Noodle Bake

This is our grandchildren's favorite.

2 cups uncooked noodles
1/2 pound lean ground beef
2 tablespoons chopped onions
2 tablespoons chopped celery, optional
1 can tomato soup
1/4 pound cheddar (or your favorite) cheese, cubed

- Preheat oven to 350^0.
- Cook the noodles in salted water for 7 to 8 minutes. Drain.
- Cook the ground beef until lightly browned. Drain well.
- Mix browned ground beef, cooked and drained noodles, onions, celery and tomato soup together.
- In a greased casserole dish, layer the noodle mixture with the cheese.
- Bake covered for 25 minutes. Remove the cover and continue to bake for an additional 10 minutes.

Janet Lamkin

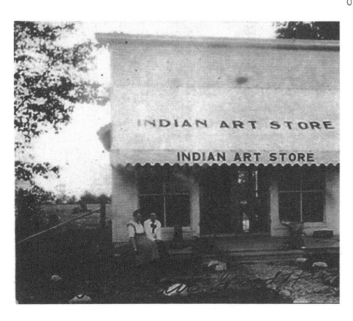

The Lamkin Indian Art Store was built on the Shore Drive, Tunnel of Trees in 1911. It featured quill worked birch bark boxes, black ash baskets and generally local Native American arts and crafts that would appeal to travelers.

Fabulous Wet Burritos

1 pound ground beef
1/2 cup chopped onion
1 garlic clove, minced
1/2 teaspoon cumin
1/4 teaspoon salt
1/8 teaspoon pepper
1 4.5-ounce can diced green chiles
1 16-ounce can refried beans
1 15-ounce can chili without beans
1 10.75-ounce can tomato soup
1 10-ounce can enchilada sauce
6 12-inch flour tortillas, warmed
2 cups shredded lettuce
1 cup chopped tomatoes
2 cups shredded Mexican blend cheese
1/2 cup chopped green onions
Guacamole
Sour Cream
Salsa

The Cross Village Hospital, built in the late 1800s by the Weikamp Convent. It survived the 1918 fire but burned in 1937.

- Crumble ground beef into a skillet; cook and stir until browned over medium heat.
- Add onion and cook until transparent. Drain off fat.
- Season with garlic, cumin, salt and pepper.
- Stir in the green chiles and refried beans until well blended. Turn off the heat but keep warm.
- In a saucepan, combine the chili without beans, tomato soup and enchilada sauce. Mix well and cook over medium heat until heated through. Turn off the heat and keep warm.
- Place a warmed tortilla on a plate and spoon a generous 1/2 cup of the ground beef mixture onto the center. Top with lettuce and tomato to your liking. Roll up tortilla over the filling.
- Spoon a generous amount of the sauce over the top and sprinkle with cheese and green onions.
- Heat in microwave for 30 seconds or until the cheese is melted. Repeat with the remaining tortillas.
- Serve with guacamole, sour cream and salsa.

Donna Wood

Four Generations

I'm proud to say I'm the fourth generation to live on this property. I grew up here, moved away, and am so happy to be back here with my husband in our retirement.

Sloppy Joes

This was a family favorite when our children were growing up. Quick to prepare, it was a great supper on nights when family members had to hurry off to evening school events.

1 pound ground chuck
1 large onion, chopped
1 can Campbell's chicken gumbo soup
1/3 cup catsup
2 tablespoons yellow mustard
1/8 teaspoon black pepper
1/2 cup hot water

- Brown ground chuck in a skillet; add the chopped onions and cook until soft.
- Add soup, catsup, mustard, pepper and hot water.
- Cook for 30 minutes.
- Serve on hamburger buns.

Bonnie Weitzel

Cuban Burgers

1 pound ground beef, made into 4 patties
1 cup mayonnaise
2 tablespoons yellow mustard
1 garlic clove, pressed
4 slices ham
4 slices Swiss cheese
4 Kaiser or hamburger buns

- Prepare grill and cook the four ground beef patties until 2/3 done to your liking.

- While the burgers cook, mix mayonnaise, yellow mustard and garlic together.

- Spread the mayonnaise mixture on the top and bottom of each bun.

- Place a hamburger on the bottom bun, top with a slice of ham and a slice of cheese. Place the bun top on each burger and individually wrap each burger tightly in a piece of aluminum foil.

- Return to the grill and place something heavy on top of the foil-wrapped burgers. (A brick or cast-iron pan works well.)

- Cook 3 – 5 minutes on each side.

- Serve with the remaining mayonnaise mixture.

Laura Ward

Tempering the Strength of Onions

When adding onions to a dish to be baked you can temper the strength of their contribution to the final dish by the way you treat them before adding. If you wish a strong taste of onions, add them chopped raw. If a medium flavor is required, the onions should be boiled whole before chopping. If a light flavor is desired, first chop then boil them.

German Burgers

1 pound ground beef
1 small onion, chopped
1 5-loaf bag of frozen bread dough, thawed
10 cheese slices of your choice of flavor
Melted butter

- Preheat oven to 350⁰.

- Brown the ground beef with the onion until browned. Set aside.

- Divide bread dough into 10 pieces. Roll each piece, 1 at a time, as flat as you can.

- As you get each flattened, place a slice of cheese and a spoonful of meat (about 1/3 of a cup) in the center and fold it up.

- Place on a cookie sheet, seam side down. Repeat for the rest of the pieces.

- Bake until golden brown.

- Remove from the oven and brush with melted butter and serve.

Katrina Aquila
Former RFC Fire and Rescue First Responder

Cross Village before the 1918 fire. Morris Mercantile is at the left. Note the plank sidewalks.

Favorite Turkey Burgers

1/4 cup thinly sliced scallions
1/4 cup finely chopped green pepper
1/2 cup finely chopped celery
3 Granny Smith apples, peeled and diced
1/8 cup canola oil
4 pounds ground turkey breast
2 tablespoons salt
2 tablespoons black pepper
2 teaspoons Tabasco Chipotle Pepper Sauce
1 lemon, juiced, with grated zest
1/4 cup chutney, pureed

- Sauté the scallions, green pepper, celery and apples in the canola oil until tender. Let cool.

- Place the ground turkey in a large mixing bowl. Add sautéed items and the remaining ingredients.

- Shape into eight large 8-ounce burgers. Refrigerate for 2 hours.

- Season the turkey burgers with salt and pepper. Place on a preheated, lightly-oiled grill.

- Grill each side for 7 minutes until meat is thoroughly cooked. Let sit for 5 minutes.

- Serve on your favorite hamburger buns.

Susan Clarke

Hot Dogs in Chili Sauce

The kids love this family favorite. We call it Grandma Beenie's Best!

2 – 3 packages of hot dogs
SAUCE:
1 medium white onion, chopped
2 tablespoons butter
2 tablespoons cider vinegar
2 scant tablespoons brown sugar
3 tablespoons Worcestershire Sauce
4 tablespoons lemon juice
1/4 tablespoon yellow mustard
1/2 cup water
1 cup catsup
1/2 teaspoon salt
1/4 teaspoon cayenne pepper
1/2 teaspoon celery salt

- Preheat oven to 350^0.
- Mix all sauce ingredients together in a saucepan and simmer for 30 minutes.
- Place hot dogs in a casserole dish.
- Pour chili sauce over the hot dogs.
- Bake for 45 minutes. Serve in buns.

Carolyn Shear

One of many local lumber camps

Blue Cheese Dogs

I've made this recipe every summer since 1966. It's so good I usually double the recipe.

6 hot dogs and buns

SAUCE:
1/3 cup sour cream
1 teaspoon instant minced onion or fresh to taste
1/4 cup sweet pickle relish
2 tablespoons yellow mustard
1/4 cup crumbled blue cheese

- Combine the sauce ingredients.
- Grill hot dogs and buns and serve with the sauce.

Maureen Mayne

Harbor Springs, Mich.

Chicago Style Pizza

This is the method developed at Pizzeria Uno in Chicago in the 1950s.

CRUST:
1 package dry yeast
1¼ cups warm water
1 tablespoon sugar
1½ teaspoons salt
4 tablespoons oil, divided
1/4 cup flour
2 tablespoons cornmeal

SAUCE AND TOPPING:
1 28-ounce can Italian pear tomatoes, well drained and chopped
1 tablespoon oregano
1 teaspoon sugar
1 pound mozzarella or Scamorza cheese, thinly sliced or shredded
1 pound mild Italian sausage, broken up, cooked and drained
1/2 cup grated Parmesan cheese

The Andrew Blackbird home and Post Office in Harbor Springs. The building was restored in 1948 as the Andrew Blackbird Native American museum.

- For crust, dissolve yeast in water. Add sugar, salt and 2 tablespoons oil.
- Stir in flour to make soft dough.
- Turn out onto a well-floured board and knead about 3 minutes.
- Place in a greased bowl; cover and let rise in a warm place until doubled, about 90 minutes.
- For sauce, combine tomatoes, oregano and sugar. Set aside.
- Brush a 14-inch deep-dish pizza pan with 2 tablespoons oil and dust with cornmeal.
- Punch down dough; press in bottom of pan. Let rise about 30 minutes.
- Preheat oven to 500^0.
- Arrange mozzarella or Scamorza cheese over risen dough. Place the cooked sausage over the cheese then spread with tomato sauce. Sprinkle with grated Parmesan cheese.
- Place pizza in the preheated 500^0 oven and immediately reduce the temperature to 450^0. Bake for 20 – 25 minutes until the cheese is melted and the crust is brown.

Jane Cardinal

Mose and Hattie Gibson ran the Blackbird Museum in the 1950s.

Morel Fettuccini with Chicken

This is a fabulous recipe for fresh Michigan morels found in late spring if you know where to look. If not, you can buy them in the area. They're expensive but worth every penny (or dollar).

2 heaping cups, cleaned and halved uncooked morel mushrooms (First trim and split the morels in half. Then soak them in salt water for several hours or overnight if possible. This loosens the dirt. Rehydrating the mushrooms also produces more morel broth during cooking.)

4 cups fettuccini

1 stick butter

1 tablespoon shallot or red onion, finely minced

1/2 cup tomato, peeled and chopped

1 cup heavy cream

2 ounces white wine

Salt and pepper to taste

4 ounces crumbled fresh Boursin cheese

1 cup asparagus or your favorite vegetable, roughly chopped (steamed)

Chopped chives, optional

Fresh herbs including rosemary and thyme or other favorites

4 grilled chicken breasts

- Cook the fettuccini in salted water and drain, leaving a small amount of the cooking liquid in the pot to keep warm. Set aside. (Drain remaining liquid before serving.)

- Heat a medium sauté pan on high until hot; turn down to medium heat.

- Add the butter and the shallots and cook until translucent. Add the morels; cook until morels are soft and all the juices have released.

- Add tomatoes, cream, white wine and drained fettuccini and toss together.

- Bring to a slow bubble and season with salt and pepper.

- Using a swirling motion while keeping the pan on the heat, crumble in the Boursin cheese and stir.

- Add asparagus or other favorite vegetable.

- Add fresh herbs.

- Serve grilled chicken on top of the pasta. Grilled salmon or steak may be substituted.

- You can also use different shapes or colors of pasta and add your favorite vegetables.

Alice Kelly

In French, chickens are named by weight. (French was the first language of our lake voyageurs and missionaries.) Poussins are baby chickens weighing from ¾ to 1¼ pounds. Poulets are spring chickens weighing from 2½ to 3 pounds. Poulardes are fat fowl weighing from 3½ to 4 pounds. Poules are boiling fowl from 4 pounds and up.

Alouette Chicken

SERVES 4

This recipe is easy and has few ingredients but it looks and tastes "fancy" because it's enrobed in phyllo dough. It's my "good company" recipe.

Chicken tenderloins
Cajun spice
Butter
Phyllo dough
Cooking oil spray
Alouette cheese spread

- Preheat oven to temperature suggested on the phyllo dough package.
- Sprinkle the chicken tenderloins with Cajun spices and sauté in butter.
- Separate phyllo dough into 8 layers and layer into a casserole dish spraying cooking oil between layers.
- Center chicken tenderloins on top of the 8 layers.
- Top with Alouette cheese.
- Fold the sides of the phyllo dough layers over the top of the chicken.
- Bake 30 minutes following the directions on the phyllo dough package.

Holly Hillier

Marmalade Chicken

SERVES 6

After accumulating many new recipes, yet still relying on old standbys, I instituted "Experimental Wednesdays" to test those in my stash. I've used this keeper for company. It would make a lovely ladies' luncheon.

3 boneless, skinless chicken breasts
Salt and pepper
3 large pitas

SAUCE:
2 tablespoons butter
1 cup orange marmalade
2½ teaspoons sesame oil
2½ teaspoons soy sauce
3/4 teaspoon hot sauce
1/2 teaspoon cayenne pepper
1½ teaspoons sesame seed

TOPPING:
1 small head of lettuce, chopped
Green onions, chopped
2 medium oranges, peeled and cut into segments
Sliced almonds, toasted

- Preheat oven to 325⁰.
- Salt and pepper the chicken breast and bake for 30 minutes.
- Cut pitas in half and open.
- Slice chicken and arrange slices in the pitas.
- Mix all sauce ingredients and heat in a sauce pan.
- Drizzle the sauce over the chicken in the pitas.
- Top with lettuce, green onion, orange segments and nuts.

Holly Hillier

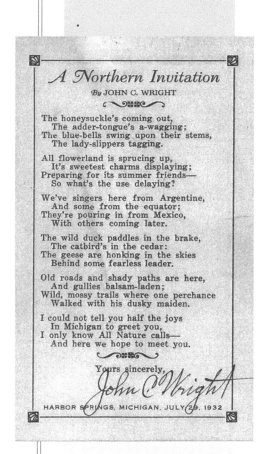

A Northern Invitation
By JOHN C. WRIGHT

The honeysuckle's coming out,
  The adder-tongue's a-wagging;
The blue-bells swing upon their stems,
  The lady-slippers tagging.

All flowerland is sprucing up,
  It's sweetest charms displaying;
Preparing for its summer friends—
  So what's the use delaying?

We've singers here from Argentine,
  And some from the equator;
They're pouring in from Mexico,
  With others coming later.

The wild duck paddles in the brake,
  The catbird's in the cedar;
The geese are honking in the skies
  Behind some fearless leader.

Old roads and shady paths are here,
  And gullies balsam-laden;
Wild, mossy trails where one perchance
  Walked with his dusky maiden.

I could not tell you half the joys
  In Michigan to greet you,
I only know All Nature calls—
  And here we hope to meet you.

Yours sincerely,
John C. Wright

HARBOR SPRINGS, MICHIGAN, JULY 29, 1932

John C. Wright was a Native American resident of Middle Village who wrote *The Crooked Tree*, published in 1917.

Chicken Artichoke Elegante

1 10-ounce package frozen spinach, thawed and
  drained
2 cups cooked long grain brown or white rice
1 egg, slightly beaten
4 tablespoons butter, softened, divided
1 14.5-ounce can artichoke hearts
1½ cups diced cooked chicken
1½ cups grated Monterey Jack Cheese
1/2 pound fresh mushrooms, sliced
1/2 medium onion, chopped
2 tablespoons flour
1 garlic clove, crushed
1 teaspoon prepared Dijon mustard
Salt
Freshly ground pepper
1 cup milk

- Squeeze spinach to remove all excess moisture.
- Combine spinach with rice and eggs in a medium
  bowl. Add 2 tablespoons softened butter. Mix well.

- Grease a 9" pie plate and press the spinach mixture into it, covering the bottom and sides.

- Cover and chill 30 – 60 minutes.

- Preheat oven to 350^0.

- Drain the artichokes and blot dry. Cut each into 2 or 3 pieces. Arrange over the crust.

- Arrange the chicken and cheese over the artichokes.

- Melt the remaining 2 tablespoons of butter in a medium skillet over low heat.

- Add mushrooms and onions; sauté over medium heat until tender.

- Stir in flour, garlic and mustard and season to taste.

- Add milk gradually. Cook until the mixture thickens. Pour over the pie. (At this point the dish may be refrigerated.)

- Bake uncovered in a preheated 350^0 oven for 45 minutes. If pie is chilled, bake for 60 minutes.

- This may be doubled and placed in a 9" x 13" casserole dish.

- Garnish with additional cheese and parsley if desired.

Christine Bommarito

Chicken Thighs Mexicano

This is a quick, easy and delicious meal. We use it with great success when entertaining folks for dinner.

8 – 12 chicken thighs
1 package taco seasoning mix
1 16 to 18-ounce jar salsa (mild or medium)
1 12 to 16-ounce jar apricot preserves
Brown rice to serve 6

- Preheat oven to 350⁰.
- Place chicken thighs in a 9" by 13" casserole dish.
- Mix taco seasoning mix, salsa and apricot preserves together.
- Pour sauce over the chicken thighs.
- Bake uncovered for 90 minutes.
- Serve with brown rice.

Jo Cunningham

The winning team! The 1912 Northern Michigan Baseball Champions of Cross Village

A Heritage Recipe . . .

Chicken au Gratin

Chickens
Noodles
Onions
Cracker crumbs
Grated cheese
Chicken broth

- Chop chicken's head off and clean the chicken.
- Stew until the bones shake off.
- Place a thin layer of uncooked noodles in the bottom of a 3-inch deep baking dish.
- Put a layer of chicken then a few slices of onions over the noodles.
- Add 2 or more layers of chicken and noodles.
- On the top layer, place cracker crumbs and grated cheese.
- Pour broth over the top and put in the oven, baking until slightly brown on top.
- Keep adding broth and bake until noodles are tender — the longer the better.
- This old recipe did not come with an oven temperature, but 350^0 seems about right.

Dolly Wyland Holland
Daughter of Than Wyland

Aunt Ruby Wyland at the Hemlock House. The Hemlock House was a popular family-owned restaurant on the Tunnel of Trees in the 1950s. Ruby was the cook and everything was simple, delicious and made from scratch.

Scaloppini al Marsala

Jack and I have always done a lot of cooking together and we love this old favorite.

1½ pounds veal or chicken scallops, sliced 3/8-inch thick and pounded to 1/4-inch
Salt
Freshly ground black pepper
Flour
2 tablespoons butter
3 tablespoons olive oil
1/2 cup dry Marsala wine
1/2 cup chicken stock, divided
2 tablespoons soft butter

- Season the scallops with salt and pepper, then dip them in flour and shake off the excess.
- In a heavy 10-12" skillet, melt 2 tablespoons of butter with the 3 tablespoons of oil over moderate heat.
- When the foam subsides, add the scallops, 3 or 4 at a time and brown them for about 3 minutes on each side.
- After they have browned, transfer them to a plate.

- Pour off most of the fat from the skillet leaving a thin film on the bottom. Add the Marsala and 1/4 cup of the chicken stock and boil the liquid briskly over high heat for 1 to 2 minutes. Scrape in any browned fragments clinging to the bottom and sides of the pan.

- Return the chicken or veal scallops to the skillet, cover and simmer over low heat for 10 to 15 minutes, basting it now and then with pan juices.

- To serve, transfer the scallops to a heated platter. Add 1/4 cup of stock to the sauce remaining in the skillet and boil briskly, scraping in the browned bits sticking to the pan. When the sauce has reduced considerably and has the consistency of a syrupy glaze, taste it for seasoning and season as desired. Remove the pan from the heat, stir in 2 tablespoons of soft butter and pour the sauce over the scallops.

Peggy Bodt

Generations in Good Hart

My family has been spending summers in Good Hart since the 1930s when Richard and Beulah Fowler, my grandparents, and their children, Forest, Marian and Jane, built two log cabins on Lamkin Road with the able assistance of Chauncey and Monnie Bliss. They called their property Legend Ledge. It was a place filled with fun and laughter, neighborhood beach fires, treasure hunts, Michigan rummy and assorted adventures. Now our grandson begins the fifth generation to continue to enjoy the simple pleasures of the lake and family get-togethers.

Beulah and Richard Fowler building the legacy of Legend Ledge

A Celebrity Chef offering . . . James Lark

In addition to owning The Lark restaurant, I have a background in Southwest cuisine. I founded the Michigan, Northwest states and Ontario chili cook-offs sanctioned by the International Chili Society. I competed in the Ontario Cookoff and in the World Chili Cookoff in the Mojave Dessert where I made it to the final table. I remain a national board member and a judge in the World Chili Cookoff. The world doesn't need another chili recipe, but most could use a foolproof recipe for barbecue ribs that can be finished either outdoors on the grill or in a broiler in the kitchen. This is a needed recipe as all but the final grilling can be done anytime earlier.

Easy Barbecued Baby Back Rib

1 rack pork back ribs, 3 pounds or less
1 tablespoon plus of Old Bay Seasoning

SAUCE:
1/3 cup commercial barbecue sauce made from tomatoes, not tomato paste, and with as little sweeteners as possible (corn syrup, molasses, sugar, etc.)
1 tablespoon red wine vinegar (Use more or less to taste.)

- Preheat oven to 300^0.
- Remove membrane from the back of the rib rack. This is impossible if the rack is too cold so remove it from the refrigerator prior to this.
- Rub the front and back of the rack with Old Bay Seasoning or your own seasoning.
- Wrap the rack tightly in heavy duty aluminum foil.
- Roast in oven for 2 hours and 45 minutes.
- If to be served more than 2 hours later, refrigerate. Keep the rack wrapped in foil and wait for it to cool before refrigerating.

The Larks in their West Bloomfield restaurant.

FINAL PROCEDURE:

- Unwrap the pork rack reserving the pork jus (juice) poured off from the foil.

- Keep the rack shaped to retain as much juice as possible when unwrapping.

- Correct the always over-sweetened commercial barbecue sauce by adding red wine vinegar to taste. Add pork juice to taste.

- Baste the bottom side and barbecue, then repeat with the top side.

- The rack may also be finished under the broiler in an oven.

James Lark
The Lark Restaurant
West Bloomfield, Michigan

Coming North

In the early 1940s my family began renting a cottage on Burt Lake for two weeks each summer, traveling there by train. College, service in the Navy and work ended my northern sojourns until I married and Mary and I began coming north. We rented a condo in the Harbor Springs area for two or three weeks each year. But in 1990 we were no longer able to find rentals that would permit our dog so we bought "our lodge" on M-119 a few miles north of Good Hart on a bluff overlooking Lake Michigan. We love our home and its location where the only commerce is the Good Hart Store and two shops.

NORTHERN MICHIGAN TROUT STREAMS.

Wolf's Pulled Pork

Pulled pork is extremely tasty when cooked properly. It is also a simple dish to prepare as you only need a few ingredients to make it great: the Meat, the Rub, a Weber-type grill (or even better a smoker with some Hickory and Apple Wood for smoking) and PATIENCE.

1 butt, cut from a pork shoulder, about 6 – 8 pounds, obtained from a butcher
Rub for the pork (see below)
Charcoal and Smoking Wood (hickory and/or apple wood)

THE RUB:
I have never measured these ingredients as I always do this by taste and in any case it is all relative, so take the amounts as guesses and only as a starting point. Taste is the ultimate arbiter for the rub. I would start with the "Basic" ingredients and taste it to make sure it's good and properly proportioned. You will want a fairly big quantity since the meat is large and there are folds where you will definitely want to rub in the mixture.
1/2 cup (or more) whole peppercorns, cracked in a mortar & pestle
Brown sugar – start with 1-2 cups, maybe a bit more
Salt to taste
1/2 – 3/4 of a regular size bottle of onion powder
1/2 – 3/4 of a regular size bottle of garlic powder
1/2 regular size bottle of oregano
1/2 regular size container of dry yellow mustard
1/2 regular size bottle fennel seed – ground in the mortar & pestle
1/2 regular size bottle ground cumin
Optional Rub Ingredients:
Red pepper, celery seed, rosemary, paprika, sage, ground coriander

Taste, Taste and then Taste some more and add whatever you think it needs. The rub can be made ahead of time if you wish.

- Put all ingredients for the rub in a large bowl and mix thoroughly. Taste. Correct the proportions of sugar to salt. Start with too little salt and then add until it tastes right.

- Rinse meat in cold water, pat it dry with paper towels and place on large cutting board. Apply the Rub liberally, and then let the meat sit for 2 – 4 hours covered, but not refrigerated.

- While the meat is absorbing the rub, soak your smoking wood chunks in water for 3 – 4 hours.

- This is where PATIENCE comes in. Prepare your Weber or Smoker for cooking while the meat is absorbing the rub.

- If using the Weber, place the coals on one side of the cooker and light them for a moderate fire. Once they're going, place a disposable aluminum "drip pan" on the other side of the grill where the meat will be. (You will want to cook the meat VERY SLOWLY at a low temperature, so don't build a roaring fire.) If your grill has a thermometer that displays the interior temperature of the grill, you will want to cook it at about 225^0 – 250^0 for several hours. At this temperature, the Butt will take about 75 – 90 minutes per pound to cook. You will have to carefully monitor the coals to keep the temperature at the right level but the amount of heat is critical and it's worth the effort.

- If you have a smoker, add 1 or 2 of the smoking wood chunks and put the Butt on the grill. As the coals burn down, add more coals (about once per hour). Every time you add coals, add a few chunks of wood.

Continued on the next page

Returning to Good Hart

I first came to Good Hart as the guest of Rhoda, Jack and Chris Herron in the mid-1960s. Since Chris was an only child, his parents often allowed him to bring a friend to Good Hart. We stayed in Rhoda and Bob Bowen's Bliss cabin on South Lamkin Road. Rhoda Herron and Rhoda Bowen were first cousins and the Bowens introduced the Herrons to Good Hart. As adults, my wife and I returned and rented in Good Hart for many years. Then in 1999, after Rhoda Bowen passed away, we bought the Bowen cabin and returned to Good Hart with our daughters.

Wolf's Pulled Pork – continued

- When the meat looks almost done, check the internal meat temperature with an instant read meat thermometer. (Checking the internal meat temperature along the way to determine the progress is also a good idea.) The internal temperature is absolutely critical to the tenderness of the meat and the "pullability" of it. I cook mine until the internal temperature is 185°.

- Remove the meat from the grill and place on a cutting board that will contain the juice that will run off the meat. Let the meat rest for about 45 – 60 minutes before it is ready to pull and eat.

- When the meat has rested, start pulling the meat off and put it on the platter for serving.

- Serve with white bread or hamburger buns and your favorite sauce on the side. Because of the terrific flavor the rub imparts to the meat, many choose not to use sauce.

Gerard Wolf

THE BEAUTIFUL SHORE DRIVE, LITTLE TRAVERSE BAY, MICH

Pork Chop Bake

6 pork chops, 3/4- to 1-inch thick
6 medium potatoes, cut into wedges
1 medium onion, cut into rings
1 can cream of mushroom soup
2 tablespoons catsup
1 tablespoon Worcestershire Sauce
1/4 teaspoon salt
1/4 teaspoon ground pepper

- Preheat oven to 350^0.
- Brown the pork chops in a large skillet.
- Place chops in a 9" by 13" baking dish.
- Mix the remaining ingredients together in a bowl.
- Cover the chops with the potato mixture.
- Bake covered for 50 – 60 minutes.

Laura Ward

Good Hart Cabins

My grandfather, Richard C. Fowler, built two cabins on the bluff along what is now known as South Lamkin Road. His collaborator in the construction was Chauncey Bliss. They built the first cabin in 1938. It has been restored and is affectionately called "the little cabin."

My parents, Jane Fowler Smith and Arthur J. Smith, Jr., spent their honeymoon in a tent on the property while the cabin was being built. Many years later, they bought a house one mile north, formerly owned by the Orth family. That property is now the site of two homes owned by my sister and brother-in-law, Peggy and Jack Bodt.

Cherry-Chipotle Grilled Pork Tenderloin

SERVES 4 to 6

2 pork tenderloins, silver skin removed

TART CHERRY MARINADE:

1/4 cup soy sauce

1/4 cup tart Montmorency cherry juice concentrate (I use Brownwood Acres brand available by order from their Eastport store or at some area specialty stores.)

1/4 cup rice vinegar

2 tablespoons honey

2 – 3 shakes of ground cayenne pepper

CHERRY-CHIPOTLE BARBECUE SAUCE:

1 or 2 chipotles in adobo, seeded and minced

3 tablespoons tart Montmorency cherry juice concentrate

3 tablespoons brown sugar

2 tablespoons black cherry preserves (such as Polaner "All-Fruit") or 1/4 cup crushed fresh cherries

2 teaspoons brown mustard

2 tablespoons tomato paste

1 tablespoon rice vinegar

1 tablespoon apple juice or apple cider

Framing-in the Foster cottage

- Place the pork tenderloins and the marinade in a large sealable plastic bag and refrigerate for 2 to 8 hours.
- Mix all barbecue sauce ingredients and set aside.
- Prepare the grill.
- Remove the tenderloins from the marinade and discard marinade.
- Sear the tenderloins over high heat then cook them over medium heat for about 25 minutes until they reach an internal temperature of 160^0.
- Glaze the tenderloins with the barbecue sauce during the last 10 minutes on the grill.
- Remove from the grill and let rest 5 minutes before slicing.
- Serve with the remaining cherry-chipotle sauce on the side.

Dorothy Livick

The Fowler cabin sits near the south end of Lamkin Road.

Pork with Applesauce Casserole

6 – 8 pork chops or pork tenderloin cut into 1½" slices
3 cups applesauce
1 package Lipton Onion Soup mix
1 can whole cranberry sauce

- Preheat oven to 350⁰.
- Cover the bottom of a flat casserole dish with the applesauce.
- Sprinkle with soup mix.
- Place pork chops or pork tenderloin slices on top of mixture.
- Spread whole cranberry sauce over the pork.
- Bake covered for 90 minutes to 2 hours. Uncover and bake an additional 30 minutes.

Marge Edwards

148—Beautiful Scene from Lake Shore Drive in Northern Michigan

A Heritage Recipe . . .

Bacon Spaghetti

This is a child-friendly family favorite that comes from my grandmother Quevenne Gatward through my mother Betty Little. We recently discovered that our friend Dave Shear's mother passed on a similar recipe to her daughter-in-law Carolyn.

1/2 pound bacon, diced
1/2 large onion, diced
1 can tomato soup
1/2 can water
1/2 pound spaghetti
Cheddar cheese, grated

SHEAR'S VARIATION:
1/2 pound bacon, diced
1 pound ground beef, browned and drained
2 medium onions, chopped
1 can tomato soup
1 28-ounce can whole tomatoes
1 teaspoon chili powder
1 pound spaghetti
Mozzarella cheese, grated

The Kelseys

- Preheat oven to 325⁰.
- Cook spaghetti according to package instructions and drain.
- Brown the bacon (and hamburger, if using) and remove to a 1½-quart casserole.
- Sauté the onion in a small amount of reserved bacon drippings.
- Combine bacon/hamburger, onion, soup, tomatoes/water and the cooked spaghetti in the casserole dish.
- Add spices if desired.
- Top with grated cheese.
- Bake for 30 minutes.

Bowties and Sausage

1 pound sweet Italian sausage
2 tablespoons olive oil
1/2 cup diced onion
1/2 teaspoon red pepper flakes
3 garlic cloves, minced
1/2 teaspoon salt
1 28-ounce can plum tomatoes, drained and chopped
1½ cups whipping cream
1 12-ounce box bow tie pasta (farfalle)
3 tablespoons minced fresh parsley
Parmesan cheese, grated

- Brown the sausage in the oil. Drain and crumble.
- Add onion, red pepper flakes, garlic and salt.
- Simmer 5 minutes then add the plum tomatoes and cook 10 minutes.
- Add the whipping cream and cook until heated through.
- When ready to serve, cook the bow tie pasta according to package directions, drain and add to the sausage mixture.
- Serve with parsley and grated Parmesan cheese on top.
- The sauce can be made ahead. If frozen, do not add the whipping cream until ready to reheat.

Marge Edwards

Lamb Shanks with Orange Liqueur

1 bottle kumquats
2 ounces Triple Sec liqueur
6 lamb shanks
1/4 cup olive oil
2 garlic cloves, pressed
3 cups beef broth
3 tablespoons tomato paste
1 teaspoon rosemary
1 bay leaf, crumbled
1 teaspoon salt
1/2 teaspoon pepper
1 – 2 tablespoons flour

The Cardinal cottage on the bluff at Blisswood

- Soak the kumquats in the Triple Sec for several hours.
- In a heavy kettle, brown the shanks on all sides in the olive oil and garlic.
- Pour in the broth, tomato paste and spices.
- Add the liquid from the soaked kumquats, reserving the kumquats for garnish.
- Cover and simmer for about 90 minutes or until tender.
- Remove the lamb shanks to a platter and thicken the sauce with flour.
- Pour the sauce into a blender and blend till smooth.
- Serve the lamb shanks on a platter with kumquats as garnish. Serve the sauce on the side.
- This is delicious over noodles.

Jane Cardinal

Lamb Moussaka

SERVES 8
3 medium eggplants cut into half inch slices
1/2 cup olive oil, divided
3 onions, chopped
2 pounds ground lamb
3 tablespoons tomato paste
1 teaspoon salt
1/8 teaspoon basil
Cinnamon
Nutmeg
6 tablespoons butter
6 tablespoons flour
3 cups milk, heated
3 eggs, beaten
1/2 cup grated Parmesan cheese
1/2 cup bread crumbs

- Preheat oven to 350⁰.

A Native American home in Middle Village formerly owned by the Gilbeault family

- Spread eggplant slices in a large baking pan. Sprinkle with 1/4 cup olive oil.
- Cover and bake in the preheated 350^0 oven for 30 minutes. Remove and set aside.
- Raise the oven temperature to 375^0.
- Heat remaining 1/4 cup olive oil in a large skillet. Add the onions and sauté until tender. Add lamb and cook until browned. Add tomato paste, salt, basil, cinnamon and nutmeg.
- Simmer uncovered over low heat until all liquid has been absorbed.
- In a saucepan, melt butter then add flour and blend.
- Cook over low heat gradually adding warm milk, stirring constantly to prevent lumping. Add some of the cheese. Add a little of this mixture into the beaten eggs, then add them into the white sauce.
- Sprinkle the bottom of a 3-quart casserole with bread crumbs. Cover with a layer of eggplant, a layer of lamb mixture and repeat layers.
- Pour white sauce over all and sprinkle with the remaining cheese.
- Bake in the preheated 375^0 oven for 50 minutes to an hour.

Jane Cardinal

Continued next page

Roast Bear with Root Vegetables

Bear season is usually in late summer or early fall so it's imperative that the bear is properly dressed, cleaned and cooled as quickly as possible. Bear meat contains tallow and thus doesn't make good steaks or burgers. I butcher mine into roasts, brats, sausage and ribs (barbecued bear ribs are a must). Treat the bear meat as if it were pork rather than beef. This recipe takes about six hours to cook.

3 pounds bear roast
Salt
Pepper
Granulated garlic
2 tablespoons chopped fresh thyme
2 tablespoons cooking oil
1 fresh apple, chopped
Onions
5 cups of water, divided
Parsnips
Carrots
Celery
Redskin potatoes
Rutabagas
Turnips

- Prepare the roast in either a cast-iron Dutch oven or a slow cooker. Use a large cast-iron skillet to brown the roast, if using a slow cooker.

- Preheat oven to 375⁰ if using a Dutch oven.

- Preheat the Dutch oven on the stovetop.

- Season the bear with salt, pepper, garlic and thyme.

- Add cooking oil to the Dutch oven and brown the roast on all sides.

- Add the apple, some large slices of onion and about 3 cups of water.

- Cover with lid and place in the preheated 375⁰ oven for 45 minutes.

- Lower the temperature to 250⁰ and cook for 60 minutes.

- Wash, peel and cut the root vegetables into large pieces including another onion.

- Remove the roast from the Dutch oven and discard the stock with the apples and onions. This will help rid the roast of any tallow.

- Replace the bear roast in the Dutch oven and add 2 cups water. Return to the oven and roast at 250⁰ for 1 hour.

- Add the root vegetables and cook another 2 hours until the vegetables are tender.

- The bear roast isn't done until it falls apart with a fork.

- Season to taste with salt and pepper.

Rich Kellogg

three years later!

Accounts of early-era community events include memories of Stutsmanville's women being great cooks. Their Ladies' Aid groups often prepared dinners to raise money for the church. Mr. Otis, of Otis Elevator fame, attended one of these dinners, and while the food may have been hot, the church was not, and Mr. Otis was rather cold. The next day he donated a furnace for the church. A new, larger chapel to accommodate the growing number of churchgoers was dedicated in 1981. The little white church, originally built between the years 1880-90, still stands next to the new chapel and serves the congregation on the corner of State and Stutsmanville roads.

Crock Pot Moose Steaks

Moose steaks

SAUCE:
1/2 cup catsup per pound of meat
1 tablespoon Worcestershire Sauce per pound of meat
Diced onions, amount to personal taste
Salt and ground pepper to taste
Brown sugar, optional

- Place the moose steaks in the crock pot.
- Mix sauce ingredients and pour over steaks.
- Cover and cook on low at least 6 hours depending on the amount of meat.

Debbie Dicken

Venison Swiss Steak

Venison steak
Flour
Sliced onions
Water

- Pound the steak, adding flour as you pound.
- Brown in a hot pan, already greased, and cover with lots of sliced onions.
- Add water to cover and simmer until tender.
- If needed, add more flour to thicken the gravy.
- Serve over pancakes.

Myrtle Kruzel Johnston

Roast Wild Duck or Goose

2 wild ducks
Oil or bacon grease
Salt
Pepper
2 small onions
1 apple
1 10.5 ounce can beef consommé
2/3 cup sherry
Flour
Water

- Preheat oven to 350^0.
- Wash ducks thoroughly and pat dry.
- Rub ducks with oil inside and out.
- Salt and pepper inside and out and rub into ducks.
- Place 1 small onion and half an apple inside each duck.
- Place in roasting pan, breast down. Add consommé and sherry and cover.
- Roast in the preheated 350^0 oven for about 3 hours, turning the ducks breast side up for the last 30 minutes.
- Make a paste of flour and water and add to the juice in the bottom of the pan for gravy.
- Salt and pepper to taste.
- Cut ducks in half lengthwise with poultry shears.
- Serve half a duck per person.

Jane Cardinal

Photo by Cliff Powers

Ruffed Grouse

SERVES 6

The end of the hunting season is best celebrated with a delicious grouse dinner. The wily grouse are so difficult to shoot; they are a rare and special feast.

3 grouse
Salt and pepper to taste
1/4 pound butter (or more)
1 small onion, minced
2 cups dry white wine
1 teaspoon tarragon
1 dash Tabasco
2 tablespoons Worcestershire Sauce
1 lemon

- Preheat oven to 450^0 or prepare grill.
- Rub grouse inside and out with salt and pepper.
- In a saucepan, melt the butter and add minced onion.
- When onion is browned, add white wine, tarragon, Tabasco, Worcestershire Sauce, salt and pepper. Cover and simmer slowly for 15 minutes.
- Strain the sauce and add the juice of 1 lemon.
- Baste the grouse liberally with the sauce.
- Grill or roast in the preheated 450^0 oven for 40 minutes. Continue to baste liberally during cooking.
- For a complete Glass family grouse dinner, serve with wild rice with currants and pine nuts, braised red cabbage, French green beans and a green salad.

Susan Glass

Jack Sanders, the beloved teller of Wind Fairy Tales

Maple-Basted Grilled Whitefish

It was common among the Algonquin tribes of the Great Lakes to serve fish with maple syrup.

1/3 cup maple syrup
2½ – 3 pounds of whitefish fillets, cut to portion size
Scant amount of ground allspice
Black pepper, coarsely ground
Salt
Corn oil to lightly oil the grilling surface

- Place maple syrup in a shallow bowl and add the fillets turning them to coat well. Sprinkle the filets with the seasonings.

- Lightly oil the grill.

- Grill approximately 6 inches from the coals, basting with the syrup until the fish is flaky and the surface is lightly caramelized.

Traditional area Native American home construction

Whitefish

"Mais la force c'est le blanc" the "poisson blanc" "The very best is the white fish."

"This fish may be called the daily bread of the fishermen on this lake; for it is, in the first place, the most abundant, and may be caught the whole year through; and then it is the most wholesome sort of fish, and has a very agreeable taste. The meat is snow-white, and, when carefully boiled, rather flaky, though never dry. You can eat it for breakfast, dinner, and supper, without growing surfeited – especially when cooked by Indian women, for they manage to serve it deliciously. Indians are very particular about their food, and this is specially the case with atikameg (the Ojibwa name of the blanc); and if it should happen to be watery, or over-boiled, the severe head of the house is sure to give the squaw a hint."

Johann Georg Kohl, 1860

Kitchi-Gami: Life Among the Lake Superior Ojibway

A Heritage Recipe . . .

Pickled Fish

Myrt's Dad, George Kruzel, was a great fisherman who ate fish all his long life of 103 years. One of the ways he fixed fish was to pickle it. It was ready to eat at any time and it kept for a good while.

Fish
Sliced onions
Salt
Pepper
Vinegar

- Boil the fish gently until just done, not mushy.
- Drain and put a layer of fish and a layer of sliced onions and salt and pepper in a crock.
- Continue layering until the crock is nearly full.
- Mix half and half vinegar and water and pour over the fish.
- Put a plate upside down on the fish and put a weight on it.
- Let it sit for a day or two and it's ready to eat.

Myrtle Kruzel Johnston

The Johnston's Royal Arch Farm

Linguine with Clam Sauce

1 dozen fresh Cherrystone clams, washed
3 cloves garlic, minced
1/4 teaspoon red pepper flakes
2 tablespoons butter
2 tablespoons olive oil
1/4 cup white wine
1 pound linguine
Fresh parsley

- Sauté the garlic and red pepper flakes in butter and olive oil in a pot.

- Add 1/4 cup white wine and reduce until about one quarter of the liquid remains.

- Place the clams in the pot, cover and watch closely. As the clams open, remove them from the pot while saving the juices in the pot. Set them aside in another bowl.

- Do not overcook the clams!

- Continue to simmer the sauce.

- When the clams are cool, remove them from their shells and chop.

- Cook the linguine, drain and toss it in the clam sauce. Add the chopped clams.

- Garnish with fresh parsley and serve.

Jack Bodt
RFC Fire and Rescue Board Member

A Celebrity Chef offering . . . John Kilborn

The Fish

John Kilborn, owner-chef of The Fish began his career as a dishwasher and bus boy at The Pier Restaurant in Harbor Springs in 1967. Almost a century before, his great-grandmother was one of the few women who survived the brutal winter of 1874-75. His great-grandfather founded the first sawmill on the Bear River in Petoskey and his Aunt Harriet established Petoskey's first bookstore, Kilborn's House of Books. John's father served as superintendent of Harbor Point.

In the early 1970s John ran Kilborn's Bakery in Harbor Springs. He then traveled and gained experience as a sous chef, executive chef and restaurant manager in Florida, California and the Midwest.

John is proud of The Fish and co-chefs who've worked with him including Randy Niswander and Greg Goodman. As one of his customers remarked, "I can't believe that the best seafood restaurant in Michigan is out here – in the middle of nowhere." (The Fish is at the corner of State and Stutsmanville roads, north of Harbor Springs.)

Crab Cakes

1/2 cup very roughly chopped parsley
1/2 loaf bread, crust removed
2 tablespoons Old Bay Seasoning
1/2 teaspoon ground white pepper
1 egg
1¼ cups mayonnaise
1½ teaspoons Dijon mustard
1½ teaspoons lemon juice
1½ teaspoons Worcestershire Sauce
1 pound backfin crab meat, drained
2 pounds claw crab meat, drained
Butter

- Preheat oven to 400⁰.
- Combine parsley and bread in Robot Coupe or food processor and process to crumbs.
- Combine bread crumbs, parsley, Old Bay Seasoning, pepper, egg, mayonnaise, mustard, lemon juice and Worcestershire Sauce in a large bowl and blend.
- Fold the crab into the mixture.
- Portion into 2 or 3-ounce cakes.
- Melt butter in a frying pan and sear the cakes on each side.
- Finish in the preheated 400⁰ oven for 5 minutes.

John Kilborn
The Fish Restaurant
Harbor Springs

Shrimp and Pasta with Smoked Tomato Marinara

SERVES 6

2 pounds diced tomatoes, fresh or canned, divided
1/3 cup extra virgin olive oil
2/3 cup chopped onions
1/4 pound small mushrooms, quartered
1 tablespoon minced garlic
2 teaspoons salt
1 teaspoon black pepper
1 teaspoon dried oregano
1 pound peeled fresh shrimp, medium size
1 tablespoon chopped fresh basil
3/4 pound dried pasta, such as penne or rotini

- Spread 1 pound of the diced tomatoes on a small roasting pan and smoke for 20 minutes in a backyard smoker or covered barbecue grill according to the manufacturer's directions.

- Set aside. (I have made this recipe without smoking the tomatoes and it was just as good.)

- In a large saucepan set over medium heat, sauté the chopped onion in the olive oil until tender. Add the mushrooms, garlic, salt, pepper and oregano and cook for 1 minute.

- Add the smoked tomatoes and the other pound of diced tomatoes and then bring the pot to a boil. Reduce the heat and simmer for 5 minutes.

- Add the shrimp and cook for about 5 minutes until the shrimp are just done.

- Stir in the basil and turn off the heat.

- Meanwhile, cook the pasta according to the package directions.

- Drain well and toss with the sauce in a large preheated bowl. Serve immediately.

Susan Clarke

Mitchell Wajigeshik, Middle Village, 1910, wearing a musk-a-mut bag of woven bark

Mother's Salmon with Biscuit Topping

TOPPING:

1 – 2 cups recipe of biscuits made from scratch or use biscuit mix

1½ cups shredded cheddar cheese

SALMON MIXTURE:

1½ cups leftover cooked salmon or 1 can salmon, skin and bones removed

1 tablespoon sautéed minced onions

2 cups medium white sauce

1/8 teaspoon celery seed

1/8 teaspoon pepper

- Preheat oven to 400^0.
- Roll out biscuit dough in a rectangular sheet about 1/4-inch thick.
- Sprinkle with shredded cheese.
- Roll up (as with a jelly or cinnamon roll) and slice in 1-inch slices.
- Mix salmon, onions, white sauce, celery seed and pepper together in a 1½ to 2-quart casserole dish.
- Top with biscuit slices and bake in the preheated 400^0 oven for 18 – 20 minutes until lightly browned.

Janet Lamkin

Grilled Salmon Balmoral

Oatmeal is one of the staple ingredients of Scottish foods, from haggis to porridge. It is often used to coat fish. My Scottish father was a great lover of any kind of fish. Salmon was a favorite in our house. My father bought the salmon at the Eastern Market in Detroit.

Salmon steaks of your choice
Flour seasoned with salt and pepper to taste
Butter, melted for frying
Medium grain oatmeal

- Lightly flour salmon steaks and dip into melted butter.
- Sprinkle oatmeal over the top of the steaks.
- Place on a buttered griddle and grill slowly on top of the stove at 170^0 for about 7 – 10 minutes.
- You can also cook in a preheated 325^0 oven for 7 – 10 minutes or till done; or cook on a grill.

Mary Groves

Grilled Salmon

1 fresh salmon fillet per person
MARINADE:
1/4 cup honey
1/3 cup soy sauce
1/3 cup orange juice
1 teaspoon garlic powder
1/2 teaspoon ginger
1 green onion, chopped, per fillet

- Mix marinade ingredients in a large sealable plastic bag.
- Place salmon fillets in the marinade and marinate for 1 hour.
- Heat a charcoal or gas grill.
- Place fillets on the grill, skin side down. Add chopped green onions and a small amount of marinade and cook for 5 – 10 minutes or until cooked through.
- The time will depend on the thickness of the fillets.

Patsy Brown

Fish Fry Batter Mix

5 pounds fish, perch, cod, shrimp or whatever you choose
Oil

BATTER:
2 cups dry batter mix (like Drake's)
2 tablespoons paprika
1 package dry ranch dressing mix
2 teaspoons Lawry's season salt

- Mix batter ingredients with enough water to make it stick to your fingers.
- Heat oil to 375^0.
- Dip fish in batter and deep fry in hot oil.

Don Horn
Chief RFC Fire and Rescue Squad and
RFC Board Member

Middle Village Church, St. Ignatius. The roof and cross had just been painted by Solomon Francis.

Recipe For:_____

_____
_____
_____
_____
_____
_____
_____
_____
_____
_____
_____
_____
_____
_____
_____
_____
_____
_____
_____
_____
_____
_____
_____
_____
_____
_____
_____
_____
_____
_____
_____
_____
_____
_____

Vegetables & Sides

Unfrozen stream near Cross Village, 1950s, by Cliff Powers

Recipes

Betty's Beans

SERVES 4

This Betty Little recipe is "the" family favorite and goes well with chicken, ham, or steak. Mom cooked these beans often for family gatherings, potlucks and picnics and after several years she finally convinced Cliff Powers to carry the "damn" beans at the Good Hart Store. Her three children continue the tradition of making these beans in Good Hart.

2 cans butter beans, well drained
1/2 stick butter, melted
2 scant teaspoons dry mustard
1 tablespoon regular molasses or 1/2 tablespoon
Blackstrap molasses
1/2 pint (1 cup) sour cream

- Preheat oven to 350^0.
- Combine melted butter, dry mustard, molasses and sour cream in a sauce pan. Cook but do not boil.
- Place beans in a casserole dish.
- Pour butter and sour cream mixture over the beans.
- Bake in the preheated 350^0 oven for 1 hour if the bean mixture is hot.
- If the beans are made ahead and are cold, bake for 90 minutes in a preheated 350^0 oven.
- Bake these uncovered but when the liquid begins to boil off, cover and continue baking.

Sally Kelsey

Creating memories at Talbot Beach, Betty (Gatward) Little shares the near-perfect joy of Lake Michigan, sand and sun with her children Bill and Sally

The Blisswood Tradition

Walter and Quevenne Gatward began their summer history in Good Hart by renting at Blisswood's Krude Kraft Lodge from Chauncey and May Bliss in the mid-1920s. Al and Betty (Gatward) Little continued the tradition renting the small Honeymoon Cabin. They moved to the larger Grey Cottage (now Bonnie and Dell Weitzel's home) as their family grew.

In 1953 Chauncey and Monnie Bliss built them a log cabin "below the hill" at Blisswood where they raised their three children, Sally, Bill and Mary during the summer. Now every year Sally and Ken Kelsey spend many months at the cabin, having raised their three children there during summer vacations. Presently five grandchildren are continuing the "Blisswood Tradition."

Cooking in Tree Bark Pots

"In cooking in bark pots, Indians heat stones and put them in the pot, and when the stones have cooled somewhat, they remove them and re-place them with other hot stones, repeating this operation until the water is boiling, and until the dishes they are pre-paring have risen to the desired degree of concoc-tion. Several witnesses in the service of the north-ern fur trade companies have assured me that by this method the Indians prepare their food very quickly."

Bishop Frederic Baraga, the first Bishop of Marquette, Michigan, served the Native American churches of L'Arbre Croche in the mid-1800s.

Baked Beans Made Easy

SERVES 6 TO 8
1 pound bacon cut into bite-size pieces
1 medium onion, chopped
1 jar Randall's Great Northern Beans
Brown sugar to taste

- Preheat oven to 350⁰.
- Cook bacon and onion together in a frying pan until done.
- Dump including the grease into a bean crock or casserole dish.
- Mix in beans and brown sugar to taste.
- Bake in the preheated 350⁰ oven for 60 – 90 minutes.

Katrina Aquila
Former RFC Fire and Rescue First Responder

216

A Heritage Recipe . . .

Three Sisters Vegetable Dish

SERVES 6
3 cups frozen corn, parched (recipe follows)
2 teaspoons oil
1 butternut squash (approximately 1½ pounds),
**   seeded and peeled**
2½ ounces dried beef or jerky
1 cup beef broth
1 cup cooked red or black beans
1/2 cup dried blueberries
Salt and pepper to taste
1/2 cup salted sunflower seeds, chopped

- To make parched corn, place corn in a large strainer and dip into boiling water for about 30 seconds. Drain. Toss with 2 teaspoons oil and place in a heavy skillet over medium to medium-low heat until the kernels are golden brown.

- Cut the squash into one-inch cubes.

- Combine squash, dried beef and broth in a medium saucepan. Bring to a boil then reduce heat and simmer until the squash is tender, about 15 minutes. Stir in the corn, beans, berries and seasonings. Cover and cook an additional 10 – 15 minutes.

- Sprinkle each serving with chopped sunflower seeds.

Native American basswood baskets used for drying berries and green corn.

The Three Sisters
The agricultural mainstays of the Ottawa:
Corn, Beans and Squash

"We believe that each one, corn, beans and squash, has its own spirit and grows well with each other. They are planted in a mound, the corn first, who is the eldest sister, who stands tall and erect. Pole beans, the third sister, are planted around the corn when it is four to five inches high, and lastly, squash is planted on the mound when her sister, the bean, has sprouted. She spreads over the ground protecting her sisters, the corn and beans, from the weeds, and it shades the soil keeping it moist."

Simon Otto, local Native American master storyteller

32A SUNSET HOUR, LAKE SHORE DRIVE, NORTHERN MICHIGAN

Greek Green Beans

Our whole family has vacationed here since the 1950s and now we live here. This recipe is an old family favorite that Mom often made as a main dish by simply adding potatoes and serving with good French bread.

1/2 cup chopped dry onion
1 clove garlic, minced
2 tablespoons olive oil
1 28-ounce can diced tomatoes
1/4 cup sliced pitted ripe olives
1 teaspoon dried oregano, crushed
16 ounces frozen or fresh green beans, thawed and
    drained or washed
1/2 cup feta cheese, crumbled

- In a large skillet, cook the onion and garlic in hot olive oil for about 5 minutes or until tender. Add undrained tomatoes, olives and oregano.

- Bring to a boil then reduce heat and boil gently, uncovered for 10 minutes.

- Add beans. Return to boiling. Boil gently, uncovered for about 8 minutes or until beans are tender.

- Transfer to a serving bowl and sprinkle with feta cheese.

Irene Hammill

Green Beans Caesar

1½ pounds fresh green beans, cut into 1-inch pieces
2 tablespoons vegetable oil
1 tablespoon vinegar
1 tablespoon instant minced onion
1/4 teaspoon salt
1 clove garlic, crushed
1/8 teaspoon freshly ground pepper
2 tablespoons dry bread crumbs
2 tablespoons Parmesan cheese, grated
1 tablespoon butter or margarine, melted
Paprika

- Preheat oven to 350^0.
- Heat beans in 1 inch salted water (½ teaspoon of salt to 1 cup water) to boiling. Cook uncovered for 5 minutes. Cover and cook until tender, 10 to 15 minutes; drain.
- Toss beans, oil, vinegar, onion, salt, garlic and pepper together. Pour into an ungreased 1-quart casserole.
- Mix bread crumbs, cheese and melted butter or margarine; sprinkle over beans. Sprinkle with paprika.
- Cook uncovered in the preheated 350^0 oven until heated through, about 15 to 20 minutes.

Bonnie Weitzel

Microwave Directions:

- Place 1/3 cup water, 1/4 teaspoon salt and the beans in a 2-quart microwavable casserole. Cover tightly and microwave on high (100%) for 8 minutes. Stir. Cover and microwave until tender, 7 to 11 minutes longer. Drain.
- Toss beans, oil, vinegar, onion, ¼ teaspoon salt, garlic and pepper together in the same casserole. Cover tightly and microwave on high (100%) for 2 minutes. Stir.
- Mix bread crumbs, cheese, and melted butter or margarine; sprinkle over beans. Sprinkle with paprika.

Bonnie (Bliss) Weitzel stands in her grandparents' garden, a testimony to the fresh produce served at the Krude Kraft Lodge, Blisswood

Stuffed Yellow Squash

If you like the taste of pizza, you'll love this kid-friendly recipe.

6 – 8 small yellow squash
1 cup onion, chopped
1/2 cup green pepper, chopped
1/2 cup tomato, chopped
4 ounces cheddar cheese, grated
1 teaspoon salt
1/2 teaspoon freshly ground black pepper
2 tablespoons basil
3 slices bacon, cooked and crumbled

- Preheat oven to 350.^{0}
- In a large stock pot, bring water to a boil. Place whole squash in the pot and boil for 8 minutes.
- Remove squash from water and let cool until you can safely handle them.
- Meanwhile mix the remaining ingredients together in a bowl.
- Cut the squash in half lengthwise and remove the seeds.
- Spoon the vegetable mixture into each squash half and bake in the preheated 350^0 oven for 12 to 15 minutes until golden brown.
- Option: if squash isn't in season, make the vegetable filling as directed above.
- Open a tube of flaky refrigerator biscuits. Separate each biscuit into thirds and place in greased mini muffin pans.
- Fill each with vegetable mixture and bake for 12 to 15 minutes as with squash halves until golden brown.
- This also makes a great appetizer.

Laura Ward

Zucchini Boats

3 medium zucchini
1 10-ounce package frozen spinach, cooked and
** drained**
2 tablespoons flour
1/2 cup milk
1/3 cup cheddar cheese, shredded
4 bacon strips, cooked, drained and crumbled

- Preheat oven to 350^0.
- Trim the ends of the zucchini and cook whole in boiling water for 10 – 12 minutes.
- Drain and halve lengthwise and scoop out the centers leaving the skin intact.
- Chop the removed zucchini pieces.
- Add to the drained spinach.
- Blend the flour and milk in a saucepan. Cook and stir until thickened.
- Place the zucchini halves in a baking dish. Salt the cavities.
- Spoon the spinach and zucchini mixture into the zucchini halves and top with shredded cheese and crumbled bacon.
- Bake for 15 – 20 minutes in the preheated 350^0 oven.

Nancy Whittingham

Zucchini-Carrot Casserole

This recipe is a favorite every year when zucchini is most plentiful. It can easily be doubled or tripled.

2 pounds (6 cups) zucchini, sliced
1/2 cup onions, chopped
1 can cream of chicken soup
1 cup sour cream
1 cup carrots, shredded
1 8-ounce package stuffing mix
1/2 cup butter or margarine

- Preheat oven to 350⁰.
- Cook squash and onions in boiling salted water for 5 minutes. Drain.
- Combine soup, sour cream, squash, onions and carrots.
- Melt butter and add half of the stuffing mix to it.
- Spread stuffing and butter in the bottom of an 8" by 8" casserole dish.
- Add squash mixture.
- Sprinkle remaining stuffing mix on top of squash mixture.
- Bake for 30 minutes in the preheated 350⁰ oven.

Bonnie Weitzel

Father Joseph Erkens and the teaching sisters of Notre Dame picnic at Good Hart. This order of sisters arrived to teach at Holy Childhood School (and later Cross Village) in 1887.

Sautéed Summer Vegetables

My grandmother, "Nawnee," made this in the summer for a lunch side dish. To her it was nothing special, just a simple way to use up a few vegetables. Nawnee and Grandpa (Dale and Bea Lamkin) had a huge vegetable garden. Grandpa fertilized the garden with manure. Nowadays that's considered "organic" gardening. My Italian in-laws call this "Gogoach." I love it because it's fresh, simple, tasty and fast!

1 medium zucchini, sliced
1 medium onion, sliced
2 tomatoes, chopped
Potatoes, sliced, optional
1 fresh garlic clove, minced
1 tablespoon olive oil
1 tablespoon plus 1½ teaspoons fresh parsley, chopped
1 tablcspoon plus 1½ teaspoons fresh basil, chopped

- Heat the olive oil in a frying pan; add the garlic and onion.
- Cook, covered until tender.
- Add the remaining ingredients and sauté until tender.

Ann E. Lamkin-Ferranti

Dale and Bea Lamkin

Hannah History

My father, John Hannah, acquired forty acres on Lake Michigan in Good Hart in the mid-1930s, before he married my mother. He often brought up the seniors on the Michigan State football teams for a weekend of camaraderie and fishing at the cottage. After he married, the cottage became a family home, the only home the family owned. My three brothers and I loved being in Good Hart all summer. We knew every nook and cranny of the woods, the old Indian trails in the woods, how to buy a coke at the Lamkin snack bar, when the mail "came in" at Cliff's store, and where the best "diving rocks" were located.

As a committed agrarian, Dad soon started purchasing farm and garden properties. He had a wonderful garden on a spectacular piece of land on the east side of Lake Shore Drive. (My brother Tom maintains the garden to this day.) And Dad purchased, little by little, almost 1000 acres of farm land around Robinson Road.

Continued next page

Ratatouille Pie

We have frequent guests in Good Hart and I like to cook things that are the essence of summer and things that are readily available in the garden.

2 medium onions, sliced
1/4 cup hot oil
2 cloves, garlic, chopped
2 small zucchini cut in 1/4" slices
3 tomatoes, peeled and chopped
1 small eggplant cut in 1" cubes
1 large green pepper cut in strips
2 tablespoons chopped parsley
2 teaspoons salt
1/2 teaspoon basil
1/8 teaspoon freshly ground pepper
3 eggs
1/3 cup cream
3/4 cup Parmesan cheese, grated (separated)
4 ounces Mozzarella cheese, grated

The Hannah children play croquet at the Lamkin Lakeshore Lodge

- Preheat oven to 400.^{0}

- Cook onions in oil in a large pan.

- Add the next 9 ingredients (through the pepper); cover and cook 15 minutes. Uncover and cook until juice thickens. (This takes a while.) Cool.

- Whisk the eggs in a bowl with 1/3 cup cream and 1/4 cup of the grated Parmesan cheese. Add to the vegetable mixture in the pan.

- Pour half of the vegetable mixture into a buttered pie plate and sprinkle with 1/4 cup grated Parmesan cheese. Cover with the remainder of the vegetable mixture and top with the remaining 1/4 cup of grated Parmesan cheese and 4 ounces of grated Mozzarella cheese.

- Bake for 40 to 45 minutes in the preheated 400^0 oven until golden.

- This may be assembled and frozen until ready to use. Defrost before baking.

Mary Curzan

His retirement project, begun rather early, was to raise cattle there in conjunction with his farms in the southern part of the state. The Good Hart farms are the basis of the generous Ed Mayne contribution to the Little Traverse Conservancy.

When the four of us started families of our own, Mother and Dad purchased the home and property above the church on Lake Shore Drive for themselves. My brother Tom lives there today. My brother Bob has the original cottage on Lamkin Road and Mike and I live on the north end of the original property.

Broccoli Casserole

This will serve 12 as a main dish if you use enough shrimp.

1 stick butter or margarine, melted
6 eggs, beaten
16 ounces cottage cheese
8 ounces English cheese, sliced and cubed
6 tablespoons flour
20 ounces chopped broccoli, cooked slightly
Optional: Add 16 ounces of cooked shrimp — the way I
like it best!

- Preheat oven to 350⁰.
- Mix all ingredients in a bowl.
- Pour in to a greased loaf pan or casserole dish.
- Bake for 45 to 60 minutes or until set.

Nancy Buskirk

Crispy Broccoli Casserole

SERVES 6 TO 8
1½ cups fresh broccoli
2 eggs, slightly beaten
1 cup cottage cheese
1 teaspoon minced onion
1/2 teaspoon salt
1 teaspoon Worcestershire Sauce
2 tablespoons cheddar cheese, grated
1/4 cup butter, melted
1/8 teaspoon pepper
1/2 cup Ritz cracker crumbs or bread crumbs

- Preheat oven to 350^0.

- Wash and trim broccoli; cook in 1/2 cup boiling water with 1/2 teaspoon salt, covered until tender crisp. Drain. Layer in a 1 quart buttered casserole.

- Mix cottage cheese, eggs, onion, salt, Worcestershire Sauce, cheddar cheese and 2 tablespoons melted butter together. Pour over broccoli.

- Add crumbs and pepper to remaining butter. Spoon over broccoli mixture and pat down.

- Bake in the preheated 350^0 oven for 30 minutes.

Holly Hillier

1920s and 30s. Chief Thundercloud (Issac Muscoe) was often on hand to create a Kodak moment for motorist visitors to Cross Village.

Spinach, Cheese and Onion Pita

Nancy is a first generation Serbian who has given ethnic cooking classes locally. She recalls that going to an American friend's home for hot dogs or hamburgers was a big treat when she was a child.

1½ pounds cottage cheese, strained or dry
1/2 pound crumbled feta cheese (or cheddar)
3/4 cup onions, chopped, slightly sautéed
Salt and pepper to taste
1 tablespoon flour, if needed
1 pound spinach, chopped
4 eggs, beaten
2 tablespoons dill or parsley
1 package phyllo dough (16 sheets)
Bread crumbs
1/2 pound butter, melted

- Preheat oven to 325^0.

Cross Village. Looking down the road to Levering. Note the four foot wood for lake steamers stacked in the foreground.

- Mix cottage cheese, feta, eggs, onions, salt and pepper together. If the cheese mixture is moist, add one tablespoon flour. Add spinach.
- To prepare the phyllo dough, use a large pan (12" by 17" by 2" or larger) to hold one sheet of dough.
- Prepare 8 layers of phyllo dough by brushing each with butter and sprinkling with 1 teaspoon bread crumbs. Place layers in pan.
- Top with cheese filling.
- Prepare remaining 8 layers of phyllo dough as with previous 8 layers by brushing each with butter and sprinkling with 2 teaspoons bread crumbs. Place layers on top of cheese filling.
- Trim any excess pastry from around the pan with scissors.
- Brush the top of the pita with melted butter.
- Bake 60 minutes in the preheated 325^0 oven until the pastry is crisp and slightly browned.
- Cut into squares and serve hot or at room temperature.

Nancy Breighner

From a Traveler's Diary: the Cross Village Dock, August, 1874

Mackinac to Traverse City. At a distance of thirty-eight miles from Mackinac, and almost within range of Skilla-gallee light-house, we "put-in" to Cross Village, a small town of say 400 people, mostly Indians. We noticed at the dock over fifty Indians, squaws and papooses, many who were endeavoring to sell the passengers their bark, sweet grass and beadwork, while others had pails full of black and blueberries, offering them at four cents a quart or fifty cents a pail full.

Vegetarian Lasagna Magro

1 32-ounce container full-fat ricotta cheese
1 cup Parmigiano-Reggiano cheese, grated
1 cup mozzarella cheese, shredded
1 large fresh egg
1/2 cup onion, chopped
1/2 pound fresh spinach, chopped
1/4 cup parsley, chopped
1/4 cup fresh basil, chopped
Olive oil
At least 1 quart of good tomato sauce
8 ounces additional mozzarella cheese, sliced thinly
4 ounces additional Parmigiano-Reggiano cheese, grated
Additional basil sprigs
1 package dry lasagna noodles

- Preheat oven to 375°.
- Mix the ricotta and 2 cups of grated cheeses together with the egg, onion, spinach and herbs.
- Cover the bottom of a large lasagna pan with olive oil and then with tomato sauce to cover. Add a little water and mix together.

- Make an overlapping layer of the dry noodles across the bottom of the pan. Spread additional sauce on top, making sure the pasta is covered.
- Add a layer of the ricotta mixture and mozzarella slices.
- Continue in this manner until you use all the pasta.
- Top with sauce and another layer of mozzarella slices, then sprinkle with the additional Parmesan.
- Cover with foil and bake in the preheated 375^0 oven for about 40 minutes.
- Check occasionally, adding boiling water around the edges if the pasta seems too dry.
- Remove the foil and cook another 10 minutes.
- Remove from oven and let rest an additional 10 minutes.
- Cut into squares and serve topped with a sprig of basil.

Susan Clarke

Harbor Springs seen from south of town in dirt-road days. At the time of this photo, horse (Indian pony) races were held starting at the church to the foot of this bluff. Andrew Blackbird's ponies often won.

Fred Ettawageshik

Spinach Polenta Gratin

This received great reviews at my first Cross Village Yacht Club potluck.

2 tablespoons olive oil
5 or more cups mixed sliced mushrooms
1 large shallot, sliced
1 pound fresh spinach leaves
1 teaspoon each nutmeg, thyme and salt
1/4 teaspoon freshly ground black pepper
1 18-ounce polenta tube, cubed
1 – 2 cups Gruyere cheese, shredded
2 tablespoons butter
2 tablespoons flour
3 cloves fresh roasted garlic
1 cup chicken stock
1 cup cream

- Preheat oven to 350⁰.

- In a large non-stick skillet, sauté mushrooms and sliced shallots until browned.

- Add spinach, salt, pepper, thyme and nutmeg and toss on high heat until wilted.

- Spread in a 2-quart casserole.

- Melt butter in a sauce pan and whisk in flour on moderate heat. Add roasted garlic then stock and cream and cook until thickened for about five minutes.

- Arrange cubed polenta on top of the spinach mixture.

- Pour sauce over and around the casserole and top with shredded Gruyere cheese.

- Bake in the preheated 350⁰ oven for 20 to 30 minutes. You may broil the top for two minutes if desired.

Annette Moriarty

Deluxe Grilled Tomatoes

This recipe is special to me because it reminds me of my father who for many years had a vegetable garden on Lots 4, 5, and 13 in Block 10 of Cross Village. Tomatoes were always one of his big crops. He planted his garden yearly from the 1930s until he was in his early 80s but in his later years the garden's size was reduced to about an eighth of an acre.

6 large, ripe tomatoes
1/2 cup seasoned croutons or bread crumbs
1/3 cup Parmesan cheese, grated
2 tablespoons butter or margarine, melted
1/2 teaspoon oregano
Freshly ground pepper, to taste

- Slice the tops off the tomatoes, cutting a zigzag edge and making a small hollow in the center.

- Drain any seeds and juice that pours out.

- Combine croutons or crumbs with the melted butter, cheese and oregano then season with freshly ground pepper.

- Spoon onto tomatoes and wrap in foil leaving the tops exposed.

- Place on grill for 10 minutes or until done.

Helen M. (Shurtleff) Cozens

An Early Cross Village Family

My family has been in Cross Village since 1870. My great grandfather, John S. Shurtleff, came to Cross Village in 1870 to be the first teacher in District 1. He later became judge of probate in Emmet County. His son Will became a merchant in the Village with a store on M-119 where he sold groceries and dry goods. His grandson, Will ("Bill"), my father, helped fight the fire on the roof of the Presbyterian Church the year most of Cross Village burned down. On December 6, 1927, my father became the rural mail carrier for the area. He retained this position until his mandatory retirement at age 70 on August 28, 1967.

Cross Village. Mary Belle Shurtleff with her family's collection of Native American Art. She holds finger woven Assomption sashes. This Native American craft was picked up by the Europeans of Assomption Quebec and were sold to the Hudson Bay Fur Co. for resale or trade. These sashes were the glory of the voyageurs.

Broiled Tomatoes

1/4 cup mayonnaise
1/4 cup Parmesan or Gruyere cheese, grated
1/4 cup shallots or green onions, minced
2 tablespoons parsley, optional
3 tomatoes cut in half

- Preheat broiler.
- Combine all ingredients except tomatoes in a small bowl and blend well.
- Gently spread the mixture about 1/4 inch thick on the tomato halves.
- Broil 4 inches from heat source for 2 – 3 minutes or until lightly browned, watching carefully so that the topping doesn't burn.
- Serve immediately. This makes 6 servings.

Linda Little

Lake Shore Drive, Cross Village, Mich.

Tomato Pudding

This recipe found in Betty Little's recipe box was from Mrs. Silian, the past owner of the Old Trail Inn on North Lake Shore Drive, north of Good Hart.

1 10-ounce can tomato puree
1/4 cup boiling water
1 cup brown sugar
1/4 teaspoon salt
1 cup fresh white bread cut into 1-inch squares
1/2 cup butter, melted

- Preheat oven to 375^0.
- Add sugar and water to tomato puree and boil for 5 minutes in a saucepan.
- Place bread squares in a casserole dish.
- Add melted butter then add tomato mixture.
- Bake in the preheated 375^0 oven for 30 minutes.

Sally Kelsey

Shore Drive
Harbor Springs Mich.

A Celebrity Chef offering . . . Bob Vala

Corn Pudding

Bread, cut in cubes (enough to fill pan halfway)
4 cups corn
1 quart cream
8 egg yolks
1½ cups sugar

- Preheat oven to 375⁰.

- Spray a 9" by 13" casserole dish with non-stick cooking spray.

- Fill casserole with cubed bread (enough to fill casserole halfway)

- Spread corn over the bread.

- Mix cream, eggs and sugar together.

- Pour over corn and bread.

- Bake in the preheated 375⁰ oven for 30 minutes uncovered and an additional 30 minutes covered until set and puffy in the center.

Bob Vala
Chef/Owner, The Crow's Nest

A vintage advertising alert for the hungry and weary that some tasty victuals were at hand

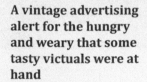

Spicy Corn Spoon Bread Casserole

SERVES 8 to 10
3 large poblano peppers
1 15-ounce can corn, drained
3 ears sweet corn (Substitute an additional 15-ounce can of drained corn or equivalent frozen corn if fresh corn isn't available.)
1 15-ounce can cream-style corn
1 cup sour cream
2 eggs, beaten
1 box Jiffy corn muffin mix (It's made in Chelsea, Michigan!)
1/2 cup (1 stick) butter, melted (Use the wrapper to grease the baking dish.)

- Generously butter a 9" by 13" baking dish or a large soufflé dish.
- Place peppers on a baking dish under the oven broiler, and char, turning frequently, until blackened on all sides.
- While peppers are roasting, shave corn kernels off cob.
- Preheat oven to 375^0.
- Cool peppers, then peel, seed and dice them coarsely.
- Mix all ingredients together in a large bowl and pour into the baking dish.
- Bake for 45 minutes or until the spoon bread sets.

Linda Bolton

A Bliss Cabin

The Bolton's Bliss cabin on South Lamkin Road was the home of the Glass family for many years. When Rick and Linda Bolton decided to remodel it and add a home office so they could spend more time up north, they immediately thought of builder Bill Glass. Bill had learned carpentry and metalwork skills apprenticing with Monnie Bliss so they knew he'd keep the integrity of the Bliss cabin heritage. That Bill had grown up in the house was a bonus. Rick and Linda now spend as much time as they can at the cabin. They enjoy welcoming younger members of the Glass family to Grandma Betty's home and like to serve this casserole to Good Hart friends.

145—Scenic Lake Shore Drive, Northern Michigan

Cheesy Rice Casserole

This is a yummy casserole from college days at Wayne State University.

2 cups cooked brown rice
2 cups Cheddar cheese, regular or reduced fat, grated
2 cups milk (whole, reduced fat, or skim)
3 eggs (or equivalent egg beaters)
3 tablespoons parsley, chopped
1/4 cup butter or olive oil
1 onion, chopped
1/2 teaspoon salt, optional
GARNISH:
Sliced almonds, toasted pine nuts or sunflower seeds

- Preheat oven to 350⁰.
- Grease or oil a casserole dish with a small amount of butter or olive oil.
- Sauté the chopped onions in the remaining butter or oil until translucent for about 3 – 4 minutes on medium heat.
- Combine with all the other ingredients (except the garnish) in the casserole dish.
- Bake in the preheated 350⁰ oven for 35 minutes or until set.
- Garnish with sliced almonds, pine nuts or sunflower seeds if desired.

Lynn Dinning
Artist & Educator
Good Hart Glassworks

Beaver Island Rice Pilaf

This goes well as a side dish with turkey breast rubbed in olive oil, lemon juice and freshly grated Parmesan cheese and roasted in the oven. It's also good with rack of lamb rubbed with pesto for an hour before placing on the grill.

1 stick butter
1/2 onion, finely diced
1 large handful of very fine egg noodles, cut into small pieces
1 cup uncooked rice
Fresh rosemary
2½ cups chicken broth

- Melt the butter in a large saucc pan.
- Add the finely diced onion and the fine noodles.
- Sauté all until the noodles begin to brown.
- Add the cup of rice and chopped fresh rosemary to taste.
- Stir together with the noodles and onion until all are coated with the butter.
- Add the chicken broth to the mixture and bring to a boil; turn heat to simmer.
- Simmer for 20 minutes or until the rice is done.
- Turn off the heat and let sit for 20 minutes.
- Cover and keep warm until ready to serve.

Cathy Vander Salm

Wild Rice
Manomin (Chippewa)

Wild rice is a seed plant, a kind of water grass and probably the most nutritive food available to Native Americans in the western Great Lakes of the past.

Near the end of August, tribal families moved to their rice camps. Each family group had its share of the rice field as was the practice in the sugar camps. These shares were staked out in tracts before the harvest season. Women gatherers sat in the sterns of canoes holding two 24-inch sticks and poling through the fields. With one stick, they bent the rice sticks over the canoe while using the other to knock the ripe kernels onto mats lining the floor of their canoes.

After drying the rice on mats, the women parched

Continued next page

Wild Rice Casserole

Native Americans used wild rice in broths containing meat, dried fruit and seasonings. Like corn, it could also be popped.

This recipe is from the home of former Michigan State Athletic Director Clarence "Biggie" Munn. It was one of his favorites and Biggie didn't get his moniker from being shy at the table.

Serves 6
1 – 1½ cups wild rice, washed at least 3 times and drained
2 teaspoons salt
3 cups boiling water
4 slices bacon, diced
1 medium onion, diced
1/4 teaspoon pepper
1 egg
1/2 cup half & half or cream
2 tablespoons butter, melted
Additional butter to grease the casserole

Native American wild rice storage

- Preheat oven to 350°.
- Add the wild rice slowly to boiling water with the salt added. Simmer 40 minutes and drain.

- Fry the bacon until crisp. Remove the bacon from the pan.
- Lightly sauté the onions in the remaining bacon fat.
- Beat the egg with the cream.
- Combine the rice, bacon, onion and pepper with the egg and cream mixture and bake in a buttered covered casserole dish in the preheated 350° oven for 40 minutes.

Biggie Munn
via Jane Cardinal

The traditional way of gathering wild rice was to pull stalks over the gunwales and beat the grain into the canoe.

it in hot kettles to loosen the hulls which they then pounded on long wooden pestles. "Trodding" on the rice completed the final husk removal. A wooden receptacle partially sunk in the ground was filled with a layer of pounded rice. A treader, wearing new moccasins, danced on the rice with his weight borne on a staff fixed in the ground. Winnowing was the last step in which the workers tossed small amounts of rice in the air until the husks blew away and the kernels fell onto large birch bark trays.

Rice was stored in woven bark bags; it was covered with hay and the bag was sewn across the top. Rice was also transported and traded in bags made of either raccoon or fawn skins. These containers were accepted as a standard measure in bargaining and trade.

Pioneer Potato Ribbons

Cut four pared, medium sized potatoes into ¾ inch slices. Pare round and round into very long ribbons. Fry them in hot lard drippings until crisp and browned. Drain on paper towels, season to your preference and serve on warmed platter. (You will find they look like roses.)

Blue Cheese Tossed Potatoes

I've taken these to Cross Village potlucks and the potlucks after the tent raising for the RFC Mini Fair.

3 pounds small new potatoes
1 tablespoon plus 1½ teaspoons butter
1½ cups green onions, chopped
1 cup plus 2 tablespoons whipping cream
1 tablespoon plus 1½ teaspoons all-purpose flour
4 ounces crumbled blue cheese
3/4 teaspoon salt
1/4 teaspoon freshly ground pepper
8 – 10 slices bacon, cooked crisply and crumbled
3 tablespoons fresh parsley, chopped

- Cook the potatoes in boiling water to cover in a saucepan for 15 minutes or until tender.
- Drain and quarter.
- Combine the potatoes, butter and green onions in a large serving bowl, tossing to coat.
- Whisk together the whipping cream and flour in a saucepan; stir in the cheese.
- Cook over medium heat, stirring constantly, until thickened. Stir in salt and pepper.
- Pour cheese mixture over potatoes, tossing gently.
- Sprinkle with bacon and parsley, toss gently and serve.

Trina Hayes

Sweet Potato Casserole

SERVES 10 to 12
4 large sweet potatoes, cut into chunks
1/2 cup sugar
1/2 cup butter
2 eggs, beaten
1 teaspoon vanilla
1/3 cup milk
Butter

TOPPING:
1/3 cup melted butter
1 cup light brown sugar
1/2 cup flour

Boarder boys laundry day at Holy Childhood School

- Preheat oven to 350⁰.
- Cook the sweet potato chunks in boiling water until tender. Drain and mash.
- Mix in sugar, 1/2 cup of butter, eggs, vanilla and milk.
- Butter a 9" by 13" casserole dish.
- Spoon the sweet potato mixture into the dish.
- Combine the 1/3 cup of melted butter, the light brown sugar and the flour.
- Sprinkle on top of the sweet potato mixture.
- Bake in the preheated 350⁰ oven for 25 minutes.

Marti Wallen

Sweet Potato Soufflé

SERVES 8 to 10

This may be assembled ahead and refrigerated or frozen. Bring it to room temperature before baking.

1 2-pound, 8-ounce can sweet potatoes, whole cut
1/3 cup sugar
1/2 cup brown sugar
2 tablespoons butter
1/2 cup milk

TOPPING:
4 tablespoons butter
1/2 cup brown sugar
1/4 cup flour
1/2 cup pecans, chopped

- Preheat oven to 350°.
- Heat the sweet potatoes in a pan over medium to low heat. Simmer until fork tender. Drain.
- Mash and add the white and brown sugars, butter and milk. Beat until smooth.
- Place mixture in a buttered (or spray with non-stick cooking spray) 8-inch casserole.
- To make the topping: melt 4 tablespoons butter.
- Mix in brown sugar, flour and pecans.
- Sprinkle over sweet potato mixture.
- Bake uncovered in the 350° oven for 30 minutes.

Sandy Kasischke

Baked Apples and Onions

We always serve this for Thanksgiving. It cooks down to less than a third of what you have to start so plan accordingly. It smells wonderful as it bakes. Everyone takes home a jar of this after Thanksgiving as it reheats beautifully and is delicious with leftover turkey.

Apples, peeled and sliced (Use one per person.)
Onions, peeled, sliced and separated into rings (Use
one small or medium onion per person.)
1 tablespoon brown sugar to each apple
Salt, to taste
Butter or margarine

- Preheat oven to 300^0.

- Butter a very large, deep casserole dish. A soufflé dish works well.

- Peel and slice an equal amount of apples and onions depending on how many people you plan to serve and how many leftovers you want to have. (I make one apple and one onion per person to have enough for leftovers.)

- Place a layer of apple slices, then a layer of onion slices separated into rings on the bottom of the dish.

- Sprinkle generously with brown sugar and sparingly with salt.

- Repeat until the dish is full. Cover with foil.

- Bake in the preheated 300^0 oven for 3 hours.

- Uncover and bake an additional 30 minutes. You can adjust the cooking time or remove it from the oven and reheat it when you need it.

Trina Hayes

Escalloped Pineapple

SERVES 8 to 10

I like recipes that I can prepare in advance with little or no last minute attention. I also like recipes with "eye" appeal especially for a buffet. This has it all including great taste and can be made a day or two in advance. It's wonderful with ham and is good enough for dessert.

1 cup butter, softened
1 cup brown sugar
1/2 cup sugar
3 eggs
4 cups cubed cinnamon raisin bread (I use brown sugar cinnamon bread.)
1 20-ounce can pineapple chunks, drained

- Preheat oven to 350°.
- Mix butter, sugars and eggs together.
- Fold in the bread cubes and pineapple chunks.
- Turn into a 2-quart buttered glass casserole dish.
- Bake, uncovered, in the preheated 350° oven for 45 minutes.

Sandy Kasischke

Baked Pineapple

This recipe is from a friend in my women's "non-bridge" group. We've gathered monthly for 30 years. For the first 15 years we played bridge until we found we had more fun if we skipped the bridge, met for dinner and just talked and shared our lives.

1 20-ounce can pineapple chunks (Drain all juice directly into a saucepan.)

1 cup grated sharp cheddar cheese or other semi-sharp cheese

1 cup sugar

2 tablespoons flour

3/4 cup (or more) unseasoned bread crumbs or cracker crumbs

2 – 3 tablespoons melted butter or margarine

- Preheat oven to 350^0.
- Mix the pineapple chunks and cheese in a glass baking dish.
- Combine the pineapple juice, sugar and flour in the saucepan. Heat to near boiling and pour over the pineapple and cheese.
- Mix the crumbs and the melted butter together and sprinkle over the pineapple mixture. You may need to increase the amount of crumbs depending on the size of the baking dish to cover all the pineapple.
- Bake in the preheated 350^0 oven for 15 – 20 minutes.

Jo Cunningham

Caramelized Onions

These freeze well with a little of the stock when poured into sealable plastic freezer bags. They're great with pork roast and with leftover turkey.

3 – 4 pounds sweet or yellow onions, peeled and quartered
1 stick butter, cut into pieces

- Fill a medium-sized crock pot with peeled and quartered onions.
- Sprinkle with pieces of butter.
- Cover and cook on low for 24 hours. Stir after 8 hours.
- Remove the caramelized onions with a slotted spoon and use the juices to make onion soup or as stock in other soups.

Trina Hayes

Cross Village, Mich.

Sweet Endings

Big Rock near Five Mile Creek, 1953, by Virgil D. Haynes
©Haynes Studio, Harbor Springs

Recipes

Crazy Chocolate Cake

My mom made this often when I was growing up. It was always on our kitchen counter so it was easy to walk by and get a "little" bite (or several)! Today, my husband John and I would love to have it every day; however, we try to limit ourselves a little more these days. It's not easy!

3 cups flour
2 cups sugar
2 teaspoons baking soda
1 teaspoon salt
1/2 cup cocoa
2 tablespoons vinegar
2/3 cup vegetable oil
2 teaspoons vanilla
2 cups cold water
Strong coffee for coffee icing

- Preheat oven to 350^0.

- Stir flour, sugar, baking soda, salt and cocoa together in a large mixing bowl. Make 3 wells in the mixture.

- In the first well, place vinegar; in the second well, place the oil; in the third well, place the vanilla. Pour the cold water over all. Mix well.

- Pour into an ungreased 9" x 13" pan.

- Bake in the preheated 350^0 oven for 30 – 35 minutes.

- This is delicious with coffee flavored icing. Make your favorite powdered sugar frosting but use strong (cold) coffee instead of water or milk.

Carlynn Booth
"Retired" RFC Medical First Responder

Family Ties

Our history in Good Hart goes back to the early 1900s when our grandfather, William Kinder, vacationed at The Lamkin Lodge. Later after renting in Chippewa Cove for many years our grandparents (William and Margaret) hired Chauncey Bliss to build a cabin on South Lamkin Road in 1935. We became full-time residents in 1998 and though the cabin left the family in 2006, we maintain our ties to Good Hart.

Reverend Dr. William Kinder, his wife Margaret and son Bill at their Good Hart Cottage in 1940

Chocolate Sheet Cake

CAKE:
2 cups flour
2 cups sugar
1 stick margarine
1/2 cup shortening
1 tablespoon cocoa
1 cup water
1 teaspoon baking soda
1/2 cup buttermilk
2 eggs
1 teaspoon vanilla

FROSTING:
1 stick margarine
1 tablespoon cocoa
6 tablespoons milk
1 1-pound box confectioners' sugar
1 teaspoon vanilla
1 cup chopped nuts

Harbor Springs, a time when the stable at the bottom right was a necessary enterprise

- Preheat oven to 375^0.
- Blend the 2 cups flour and 2 cups sugar together and set aside.
- Combine 1 stick margarine, 1/2 cup shortening, 1 tablespoon cocoa and 1 cup water in a saucepan and bring to a boil.
- Pour over the flour and sugar mixture and mix well.
- Add the baking soda, buttermilk, eggs and 1 teaspoon of vanilla and mix together.
- Pour into a 16" x 11" jelly roll pan and bake in the preheated 375^0 oven for 20 minutes.
- Cool the cake for 10 minutes.
- Spread with the frosting.

FROSTING:

- Combine 1 stick margarine, 1 tablespoon cocoa and 6 tablespoons milk in a saucepan and bring to a boil.
- Add the powdered sugar and mix well.
- Add 1 teaspoon vanilla and 1 cup chopped nuts.

Georgie Richner

Chocolate Bar Cake

CAKE: (You may also use Duncan Hines German Chocolate cake mix.)

2 cups sugar

2 sticks (1 cup) butter or margarine

1 teaspoon vanilla

2 eggs

2½ cups cake flour

1 cup cocoa

2 teaspoons baking soda

1/2 teaspoon salt

2½ cups buttermilk

FROSTING:

1 8-ounce package cream cheese, softened

1 cup powdered sugar

1/2 cup granulated sugar

10 1.5-ounce Hershey milk chocolate bars with almonds

1 12-ounce container whipped topping

- Preheat oven to 350^0.
- Grease and flour 3 round cake pans 9" x 1½".
- Beat sugar, butter and vanilla in a large bowl with an electric mixer on medium speed until light and fluffy. Beat in the eggs, 1 at a time.
- Mix the cake flour, cocoa, baking soda and salt together.
- Beat the flour mixture into the sugar mixture alternating with the buttermilk on medium speed. Beat an additional minute after adding all the ingredients then pour the mixture into the 3 prepared cake pans.
- Bake 30 minutes in the preheated 350^0 oven until a cake tester inserted in the center comes out clean. Cool 10 minutes. Remove cake layers from the pans to a wire rack. Cool completely.
- While the cake cools, prepare the frosting. Beat the cream cheese, powdered sugar and granulated sugar on medium speed with a mixer until creamy.
- Finely chop 8 of the candy bars. Fold the cream cheese mixture and the chopped candy bars into the whipped topping.
- Spread the frosting between the layers and on top and sides of the cake.
- Chop the remaining 2 candy bars and sprinkle half of the candy on top of the cake. Press the remaining half along the bottom edge of the cake.

Joan Craven

Fred Ettawageshik, a graduate of the Carlisle Institute, Pennsylvania. Fred and his wife, anthropologist Jane Ettawageshik, wrote *The Art of Tradition* with Gertrude Kurath. Fred owned a Native Art shop in Harbor Springs.

OTTAWA INDIANS
Harbor Springs, Mich.

Mounds Cake

1 chocolate devil's food cake mix
FROSTING:
24 large marshmallows
1 cup milk
1 cup sugar
1 teaspoon vanilla
1 14-ounce package coconut
1½ cups sugar
1 stick butter or margarine
1/2 cup milk
1 12-ounce package chocolate chips

- Bake the cake according to the package directions.
- For the frosting, in a saucepan mix the marshmallows, milk, sugar and vanilla. Heat and stir until melted.
- Remove from heat, stir in the coconut and set aside.
- In another saucepan, mix sugar, butter or margarine and milk and bring to a boil.
- Remove from heat; add chocolate chips, stirring until melted.
- Spoon the coconut mixture evenly over the warm cake.
- Pour the chocolate mixture over the coconut mixture.
- Chill the cake in the refrigerator to help set the frosting.

Barb Rice

Aunt Blanche's Chocolate Bittersweet Icing

This makes a very good soft icing.

2 1-ounce unsweetened baking chocolate squares
1 tablespoon plus 1½ teaspoons cornstarch
3 tablespoons cold water
1/2 cup sugar
1/2 cup boiling water
1/8 teaspoon salt
1 teaspoon vanilla
1½ teaspoons butter

- Melt chocolate over low heat in a saucepan or double boiler.
- In a small bowl, dissolve the cornstarch in 3 tablespoons of water, and set aside.
- Mix the sugar with the boiling water.
- Add the sugar and water mixture to the chocolate.
- Then add the cornstarch mixture and salt.
- Bring to a boil, stirring constantly, until thickened.
- Remove from heat and stir in the vanilla and butter.
- Spread the warm frosting on a cake or cupcakes.
- Place in the refrigerator to set up.

Wortley Family

Photo by Harriet Jackson

The Good Hart Bible Church

Maude Sterly was eight years old when she first attended the Good Hart Bible Church. She's in her late 80s now, and it's been her church ever since.

The small white wooden house of worship has stood at the corner of Church and Middle Village roads for well over 100 years. In the early days, it was a missionary church. Maude remembers a man of the cloth would "travel through the area and hold religious meetings and folks would come to hear him." Maude's father and mother, Jack and Ruby Kidder, were long-time congregants and Jack's grandparents furnished the logs for the church.

At one time, its affiliation was Christian Assembly, then Baptist, then Methodist. For a while, the church closed. Through the years, membership grew, slacked off, and then grew again. "During the days when a lot of people were coming to church the congregation decided to buy the building from the Methodist Church for about $700." Later, the church built a parsonage. "Those were hard times, and people used whatever they had, like old two-by-fours."

Pastor Rodney Ward and his wife Mabel led the church in the 1960s at a time when the belfry needed repair. "We took out the copper bell and put it on the ground. It got stolen." Mrs. Ward wrote an article to the newspaper and "pleaded that the bell be returned, no questions asked. All of a sudden, the bell was back."

In 2006, an addition was put on. "And we got indoor toilets which was really nice."

Maude describes the Good Hart Bible Church today as independent Christian. Through its long history, more than enough hard-working folks have ensured its longevity. "We live in the country, you know. The church holds us together."

Note: Maude Valeria (Kidder) Sterly died on October 26, 2012, just a short time after sharing this history of her church.

A Heritage Recipe...

Maude's Feather Cake

I usually frost this cake with a powdered sugar icing.

2 cups flour
1 cup sugar
1/2 cup shortening
2 eggs
1 cup milk
3 – 4 teaspoons baking powder
Dash salt (1/4 teaspoon)
1 teaspoon vanilla

- Preheat oven to 350^0.
- Combine all ingredients in a large mixing bowl. Beat until smooth. Beat for another minute. The batter will be very thick.
- Grease and flour two 8-inch layer pans.
- Divide the batter into the pans.
- Bake for 25-30 minutes until the center springs back to the touch.

Maude Sterly

Andrew J. Blackbird, who worked to protect the treaty rights of the Anishinabe people

Black Bottom Cupcakes

MAKES 18 CUPCAKES

CAKE:
1½ cups flour
1 cup sugar
1/4 cup cocoa
1 teaspoon baking soda
1/2 teaspoon salt
1 cup water
1/3 cup oil
1 tablespoon white vinegar
1 teaspoon vanilla

FILLING:
1 8-ounce package cream cheese at room temperature
1 egg
1/3 cup sugar
1/8 teaspoon salt
1 cup semi-sweet chocolate chips

- Preheat oven to 375⁰.
- Mix all cake ingredients in a large bowl.
- Mix all filling ingredients in a small bowl and set aside.
- Line cupcake pans with cupcake paper liners.
- Fill each cupcake tin 2/3 full of cake batter.
- Top each cupcake with a generous teaspoon of the filling mixture.
- Bake for 30 minutes.
- There is no need to frost these.

Linda Little

Banana Cake with Butter Frosting

CAKE:
2/3 cup butter
1⅔ cups sugar
2½ cups flour
1¼ teaspoons baking powder
1 teaspoon baking soda
1 teaspoon salt
1¼ cups mashed bananas (about 3 bananas)
2/3 cup buttermilk
2 eggs

FROSTING:
1 stick butter, softened
1 teaspoon cream
1 teaspoon vanilla
2 cups powdered sugar

- Preheat oven to 350⁰.
- Cream 2/3 cup butter together with 1²/₃ cups sugar.
- Stir in flour, baking powder, baking soda and salt.
- Add mashed bananas and 1/3 cup buttermilk and beat for 2 minutes.
- Add 1/3 cup remaining buttermilk and the 2 eggs.
- Beat thoroughly.
- Pour into a greased and floured 9" x 13" pan.
- Bake in the preheated 350⁰ oven for 40 – 45 minutes. Cool.
- For the frosting mix butter, cream, vanilla and powdered sugar together until smooth.
- Spread frosting on the cooled cake.

Pat Dobson

This recipe is from a dear friend, and every time I make this cake, I have fond memories of her. It was one of my son Blake's favorite desserts when he was growing up and it still is.

The Middle Village home of Tom King, the last Odawa headman of the Village

Carrot Cupcakes

MAKES 12 CUPCAKES

CUPCAKES:
1 cup sugar
1/3 cup vegetable oil
2 tablespoons orange juice
1/2 teaspoon vanilla
2 large eggs
1 teaspoon baking powder
1/2 teaspoon baking soda
1/2 teaspoon ground allspice
1/2 teaspoon salt
3/4 cup + 2 tablespoons flour
1½ cups shredded carrots
1/2 cup chopped walnuts
1/4 cup shredded coconut

CREAM CHEESE ICING:
1 8-ounce package cream cheese, softened to room temperature
3/4 cup confectioners' sugar
1/4 teaspoon vanilla

Shredded coconut, toasted

- Preheat oven to 350^0.
- In a bowl combine the sugar, oil, orange juice, vanilla and eggs.
- Stir in the baking powder, baking soda, allspice and salt. Add the flour and mix.
- Stir in the shredded carrots, walnuts and coconut.
- Insert 12 paper cupcake liners in muffin pan. Distribute the batter evenly.
- Bake in the preheated 350^0 oven for 25 minutes. Cool before frosting.
- To make the frosting whisk the cream cheese, confectioners' sugar and vanilla until smooth.
- Garnish frosted cupcakes with toasted shredded coconut.

Debbie Dicken

This image was drawn from a photo by Debbie Dicken of a nest of robins near her Cross Village cottage.

Along the Tunnel of Trees, below a hill just south of Good Hart, the bright white steeple of St. Ignatius points skyward, well above the treetops.

By 1741, Jesuit missionaries were making their way across Lake Michigan in birch bark canoes, where they established the first mission church in Middle Village along the area known as L'Arbre Croche. Oral history describes the first chapel in honor of Ignatius of Loyola as a bark-covered longhouse centrally located in this thriving Indian village. The first priest, Father Pierre-Luc du Jaunay, served the Odawa people until 1765.

In 1825, a second and larger church was built one mile north. Enlarged in 1833, it was dedicated by Bishop Frederic Baraga. By 1866, a new church was erected and it looked much like the St. Ignatius of today. Two decades later this wooden structure was destroyed by a chimney fire.

Today's church, built by
Continued next page

Cherry Pudding Cake

This favorite was made frequently by Dick's mother, Fay Guyor, who vacationed with us in Good Hart every year from 1970 until her death. She always vacationed at a family cottage in the Traverse City area as well and learned to love making desserts with cherries.

CAKE:
1/3 cup shortening
2/3 cup sugar
1 egg
1/3 cup milk
1/2 teaspoon vanilla
1/2 teaspoon lemon extract
1/8 teaspoon salt
1½ cups flour
2 teaspoons baking powder
1/2 cup drained tart cherries

SAUCE:
2/3 cup sugar
2 tablespoons flour
1/8 teaspoon salt
1 cup water
2 tablespoons butter
2 tablespoons lemon juice
2/3 cup canned cherries and juice

Whipped cream, optional

Old markers in the St. Ignatius churchyard

- Preheat oven to 350⁰.
- Cream the shortening and sugar together. Add the egg, milk, vanilla, lemon extract, salt, flour and baking powder and beat for 2 minutes.
- Pour into a greased 8" x 8" shallow pan.
- Dot with cherries on top.
- Bake for 25 minutes in the preheated 350⁰ oven.
- Combine the sauce ingredients in a saucepan. Cook over medium heat, stirring constantly until thickened.
- Serve it warm over cut squares of cake.
- Top with whipped cream if desired.

Stephanie Guyor

local Native Americans immediately following the 1889 fire, is the third to stand on the present site. The new foundation sits atop the old; inside, the walls are embossed tin. The steeple bell is marked 1889. Mass is celebrated during summer months.

Alongside the church is an historic Odawa cemetery. Row upon row of graves follows the gentle slope of the dune. As is the custom, each burial site is marked with a simple white cross. Several are decorated with flowers, ribbons, American flags and an occasional dream catcher.

CHURCH AT MIDDLE VILLAGE, GOOD HART, MICHIGAN   20127

My husband, Allan, grew up in Harbor Springs. I first came to the area in the early 1960s and Allan's and my favorite beach was in Good Hart. Allan's job took us all over the country but we told his parents to let us know if beach property was ever up for sale. In 1974 they called about property for sale in Good Hart. We said we'd take it.

It so happened that the sellers were Anne and Ed Burt. Anne's parents had a cottage next to the property we were purchasing and Allan had been there many times as a child. Allan and Anne were next door neighbors as children in Harbor Springs. To make our purchase even better, after we moved to Good Hart permanently in 1997, Anne and Ed built a home right next to us and became our neighbors.

Pineapple Cake

This recipe was given to me by an aunt, Ruth Allerding. It makes a nice, moist cake.

CAKE:
2 eggs
1 20-ounce can crushed pineapple with juice
2 cups flour
1 cup white sugar
1 cup brown sugar
2 teaspoons baking soda

FROSTING:
1 stick butter, softened
1 8-ounce package cream cheese, softened
1 teaspoon vanilla
2 cups sifted powdered sugar

- Preheat oven to 350⁰.
- Mix eggs, pineapple, flour, white and brown sugar and baking soda together. Pour into an ungreased 9" x 13" pan.
- Bake for 40 – 45 minutes.
- For the frosting mix the butter, cream cheese and vanilla together.
- Beat in the sifted powdered sugar and frost the cake.

Patti Allerding

The smokey-eyed, glamorous Zelphia DeWitt was Anne Burt's mother. Zelphia had been a roommate of vintage film star Zazu Pitts before becoming a teacher in Harbor Springs.

Pumpkin Raisin Sheet Cake

CAKE:
2 cups all-purpose flour
2 cups sugar
2 teaspoons baking powder
1 teaspoon baking soda
1 teaspoon cinnamon
1 teaspoon nutmeg
1/2 teaspoon salt
1/2 teaspoon ground cloves
1 cup oil
4 eggs
1 15-ounce can (2 cups) pumpkin
1/2 cup chopped nuts
1/2 cup raisins

FROSTING:
1/3 cup softened butter or margarine (I use part sour
  cream.)
1 3-ounce package cream cheese, softened
2 cups powdered sugar
1 tablespoon milk
1 teaspoon vanilla

- Preheat oven to 350^0.
- Combine all ingredients except nuts and raisins in a large bowl and beat at low speed until moistened. Beat at medium speed for 2 minutes. Stir in the nuts and raisins.
- Spread in a greased 15" x 10" x 1" jelly roll pan.
- Bake for 25 – 30 minutes.
- To make the frosting combine the butter (and sour cream, if used), cream cheese, powdered sugar, milk and vanilla.
- Cool the cake completely before frosting.

Rosemary Stolt

Stolt Haus

Our family has a strong, sentimental attachment to our home on Townline Road. Albert and Ethel Stolt built it in the early 1930s by disassembling three other buildings for the building supplies. My husband, Edwin, was born in this house in 1935. Albert died of pneumonia in 1936 before the house was completed. When Ed was four, he moved with his mother and sister to town as Ethel had married Lloyd Fisher. The house was rented for a time and Ed's sister and family lived in it in the summers when their family was young. Ed began rebuilding the house in 1969. It was in great disrepair and Ed was fairly new at carpentry. We moved in with our two daughters in October, 1970. There are a few things we would change but we do love our place. The only way I'm leaving Stolt Haus is in a pine box.

265

Great Pumpkin Dessert Cake

1 15-ounce can solid pack pumpkin
1 12-ounce can evaporated milk
3 eggs
1 cup sugar
4 teaspoons pumpkin pie spice
1 18¼–ounce yellow cake mix
3/4 cup butter or margarine, melted
1½ cup chopped walnuts
Vanilla ice cream or whipped cream

- Preheat oven to 350^0.
- In a mixing bowl, combine the pumpkin, evaporated milk, eggs, sugar and pumpkin pie spice.
- Put in a greased 9" x 13" baking pan.
- Sprinkle the dry cake mix over the mixture.
- Drizzle the melted butter over the top.
- Top with chopped walnuts.
- Bake for 1 hour. Serve with ice cream or whipped cream.

Don Horn
Chief, RFC Fire and Rescue Squad and
RFC Board Member

Rhubarb Shortcake

This is wonderful when made with Pond Hill Farm's fresh rhubarb.

1 cup sugar
1 cup flour
3/4 cup light cream or milk
1 teaspoon baking soda
1 cup cubed rhubarb

- Preheat oven to 325^0.
- Mix all ingredients and pour into a greased loaf pan.
- Bake for 40 minutes or until browned on the top.
- Serve in a dish with milk.

Caroline Smith Lewis

Early days in Cross Village

Torta Crema
(Italian Crème Cake)

1 stick unsalted butter, softened
1/2 cup vegetable shortening
2 cups sugar
5 eggs, yolks separated from whites
2 cups flour
1 teaspoon baking soda
1 cup buttermilk
1 teaspoon vanilla
1 cup flaked coconut
1 cup chopped pecans

- Preheat oven to 350°.
- Cream the butter and shortening; add the sugar and beat some more. Add the egg yolks and beat.
- Mix the flour and baking soda and add alternately to the butter mixture with buttermilk.
- Stir in the vanilla, coconut and pecans.
- Beat egg whites until stiff and fold into the cake mixture.
- Pour the batter into 3 well-greased round cake pans or a 9" x 13" x 2" baking pan.
- Bake for 40 – 45 minutes (until a stick of dry spaghetti inserted in the middle comes out clean). Cool before frosting with your favorite icing.

Susan Clarke

Peg's Cheesecake

1/2 stick (4 tablespoons) butter plus additional for the sides of the pan
9 crushed graham crackers plus additional for the sides of the pan
2 8-ounce packages cream cheese, softened
3/4 cup sugar
3 eggs
16 ounces (2 cups) sour cream
1 teaspoon vanilla

- Preheat oven to 375⁰.
- Butter the sides of a springform pan.
- Melt the butter and mix with 9 crushed graham crackers. Press into the bottom of the springform pan.
- Sprinkle crushed graham crackers onto the buttered sides of the pan.
- Blend the cream cheese with the sugar. Add the eggs 1 at a time, mixing well after each addition.
- Add the sour cream and vanilla and beat well for 2 – 3 minutes.
- Bake for 30 minutes.
- Turn off the oven. Leave the oven door closed and leave the cake in the oven for 1 hour.
- Open the oven door and let the cake cool completely.
- Chill. Before serving let the cheesecake sit out for about an hour.
- This is especially good with fresh strawberries.

Peggy Bodt

Late in life Andrew Blackbird posed for souvenir photos for resorters. In his working years he served in a number of government positions. Suits were his common attire.

Chocolate Grand Marnier Cheesecake

CRUST:
1 cup graham cracker crumbs
1/2 cup finely chopped almonds
1/2 cup shortbread crumbs
1/4 cup butter, melted

FILLING:
3 8-ounce packages (1½ pounds) cream cheese, softened
16 ounces sour cream
3/4 cup sugar
3 eggs
1/2 teaspoon vanilla
Zest of 1 lemon

TOPPING:
5 ounces semi-sweet chocolate (not chips)
2 ounces Grand Marnier

The postcard caption says it all.

- Combine graham cracker crumbs, almonds, shortbread crumbs and melted butter and press into the bottom of a 9" springform pan and freeze.
- Preheat oven to 290^0.
- Combine filling ingredients and pour part over crust to form a 1/2-inch layer.
- Melt the semi-sweet chocolate with the Grand Marnier in a double boiler.
- Mix the melted chocolate mixture with the remaining cream cheese mixture and pour into the springform pan.
- Bake in the preheated 290^0 oven for 90 minutes.
- Freeze overnight and cut while partially frozen for clean edges.

John Kilborn
Chef/Owner The Fish Restaurant

The Little children in their shoreside cottage. Bill, on the left, married Linda.

Bavarian Apple Torte

CRUST:
1/2 cup butter
1/3 cup sugar
1/4 teaspoon vanilla
1 cup flour

FILLING:
1 8-ounce package cream cheese, softened
1/4 cup sugar
1 egg
1/2 teaspoon vanilla

TOPPING:
4 cups apples, peeled, cored and thinly sliced
1½ teaspoons cinnamon
1/3 cup sugar
1/4 cup sliced almonds

- Preheat oven to 450⁰.
- Mix crust ingredients and pat into a 9" springform pan.
- Mix filling ingredients and spread over the crust.
- Mix topping ingredients and spread on top of the filling.
- Bake in the preheated 450⁰ oven for 10 minutes.
- Reduce heat to 400⁰ and bake an additional 25 minutes.
- Serve warm or at room temperature.

Linda Little

Rhubarb Torte

1 cup flour
1/2 cup butter, softened
5 tablespoons powdered sugar
1/8 teaspoon salt
2 eggs
1½ cups sugar
1/4 cup flour
3/4 teaspoon baking powder
3 cups cubed rhubarb

- Preheat oven to 375⁰.
- Mix the 1 cup flour, softened butter, powdered sugar and salt together and pat into an 8" x 8" pan.
- Bake for 10 minutes.
- Mix the eggs, sugar, 1/4 cup flour and baking powder together. Fold in the rhubarb.
- Pour over the hot crust.
- Bake an additional 35 – 40 minutes or until slightly browned on top.

Caroline Smith Lewis

Lemon Meringue Pie

This is my mother-in-law Hilda Allerding's recipe. She came to Harbor Springs as a young woman with a family from St. Louis that spent their summers in Wequetonsing. She met and married Asa Allerding and they owned the City Grocery on the corner of Main and State Streets in Harbor Springs. Every time Hilda brought this pie to a club meeting, Patsy Ketterer's column in the local paper would note that Hilda Allerding had served her famous lemon pie.

1 baked 9" pie crust

FILLING:
6 tablespoons cornstarch
1½ cups sugar
1/4 teaspoon salt
1/3 cup cold water
2/3 cup fresh lemon juice
3 egg yolks, beaten
2 tablespoons butter
1½ cups boiling water
1 teaspoon lemon rind, grated

MERINGUE:
3 egg whites
1/4 teaspoon cream of tartar
4 tablespoons sugar, divided

- Preheat oven to 350^0.
- Sift the cornstarch, 1½ cups sugar and salt together.
- Combine cold water and lemon juice in a medium saucepan. Whisk in the cornstarch mixture and cook over medium heat stirring constantly until the mixture starts to thicken.
- Whisk a small amount of the warm filling into the beaten egg yolks to prevent curdling. Add the remaining egg mixture and boiling water to the saucepan. Bring to a full boil, stirring constantly as it thickens; reduce heat and simmer 1 minute.
- Remove from heat and add 1 teaspoon of grated lemon rind.
- Pour into the prepared pie shell.
- To make the meringue, beat the egg whites and cream of tartar until soft peaks form.
- Add 3 tablespoons sugar while still beating until stiff peaks form.
- Spread meringue on the pie to the edges of the crust so the meringue doesn't shrink.
- Before baking sprinkle 1 tablespoon sugar over the meringue for easy cutting.
- Bake the pie in the preheated 350^0 oven for 10 – 15 minutes.

Patti Allerding

Asa Allerding outside his Harbor Springs grocery

Sour Cream Lemon Pie

Beth Ann Burns and I served this at an Extension Club meeting and everyone begged for the recipe.

CRUST:
1¼ cup crushed graham cracker crumbs
2 tablespoons sugar
1/4 cup melted margarine or butter

FILLING:
1 cup sugar
1/4 cup cornstarch
1 cup milk
3 egg yolks, slightly beaten
1/3 cup fresh lemon juice
1/4 cup margarine or butter, cut into small pieces
1 tablespoon lemon peel, grated
1 cup (8-ounce container) sour cream

Whipped Cream for topping
Lemon peel for garnish

- Preheat oven to 350⁰.
- Mix crust ingredients and press into a 9" pie pan.
- Bake for 6 minutes. Cool.
- For the filling combine the sugar, cornstarch, milk and the slightly beaten egg yolks in a saucepan.
- Cook, stirring, over medium heat until thick and bubbly. Cook an additional 2 minutes.
- Remove from heat. Gently stir in the lemon juice, margarine or butter and the lemon peel.
- Gently fold in the sour cream until combined.
- Top with whipped cream and garnish with lemon peel.

Harriet Jackson

Easy Lemonade Pie

When cutting the pie, I rinse my knife with warm water between each cut so the pie doesn't stick to the knife.

Graham cracker crust (or baked pie crust)
1 14-ounce can sweetened condensed milk
1 6-ounce can lemonade concentrate, thawed
1 8-ounce container Cool Whip whipped topping, thawed

- Mix the condensed milk and lemonade together. Fold in the whipped topping.
- Pour into the graham cracker crust and freeze until set.
- This is delicious when topped with fresh strawberries or blueberries.

Laura Ward

Blueberries

Minan: the First Fruit of the Anishinabeg

There is an Anishinabeg saying that the family that dries the most minan in August, the month of the blueberry moon, will be the healthiest in the spring. Blueberries dry in the sun in about 10 days and are ready to pack in makaks. The birch bark makaks resist rot and when lined with tallow provide near perfect storage.

During maple syrup-making season, Native American families had little time to cook. It was too hard to interrupt the syrup-making process. An early energy drink made of dried blueberries and slightly thickened maple syrup, whisked with a sassafras whisk, staved off hunger. Blueberries

Continued next page

Blueberry Delight

When my two daughters were little we spent many a July morning picking wild blueberries out by the old Cross Village dump. The berries that weren't gobbled by the girls were used for this dessert. We picked berries all summer. In July we also made pies from the fruit of the Juneberry trees. In July and August we used wild raspberries for jam. In August and September we picked blackberries for their Dad's "Blackberry Burp," a liqueur made from vodka, sugar and blackberries that aged for six months in a big jar in the crawl space under our house. In September we made applesauce from apples in the area's abandoned orchards. I continue to enjoy hunting and gathering with my grandchildren.

1 recipe for graham cracker crust
1 16-ounce container whipped topping
1 14-ounce can sweetened condensed milk
1/3 cup fresh lemon juice
1 – 1½ quarts fresh blueberries
1/2 cup chopped pecans, optional

- Prepare the graham cracker crust mixture and press into the bottom of a greased 9" x 13" pan. Chill until firm.

- Mix the whipped topping, condensed milk and lemon juice. Fold in the blueberries.

- Spread in the prepared dish and sprinkle with pecans if desired.

- Chill until ready to serve.

Anne Munger

Blueberry Streusel

3/4 cup flour
1 cup brown sugar
1 stick butter, softened
4 cups blueberries

- Preheat oven to 350^{0}.
- Cream the flour, brown sugar and butter together.
- Place blueberries in an 8" x 8" pan. Sprinkle the flour, sugar and butter mixture over the blueberries.
- Bake for 40 minutes.
- Serve with vanilla ice cream.

Mary Curzan

are rich in calcium, phosphorus, iron and vitamin C. Dried blueberries are mold resistant and thus can be stored well.

Local corn meal was made from versicolored corn pounded in a poo-ta-gan. To make a favorite treat, cornbread dough was filled with dried blueberries then shaped into bannocks (small cakes), laid on a maple plank and baked by a fire. Breaking open a warm bannock and pouring in a little maple syrup made them even better.

Grandmother's Blueberry or Huckleberry Pie

This was Sarah Hannah's recipe. John Hannah grew the blueberries and she often made these pies. We think that her housekeeper at Juniper Lodge on Lamkin Road gave her the recipe in the 1940s. The huckleberry is similar to the blueberry but its seeds are larger.

FILLING:
5 cups blueberries or wild huckleberries
1 cup sugar
1 tablespoon minute tapioca

CRUST:
1 heaping tablespoon butter, softened
1 heaping tablespoon sugar
1 egg
1 cup flour
1 heaping tablespoon baking powder

Powdered sugar, sifted

- Mix the berries, 1 cup sugar and tapioca together in a large bowl. Crush about half of the berries and let sit for about 15 minutes.
- Preheat oven to 375°.
- Cream the butter and heaping tablespoon of sugar together. With a fork, beat the egg into the creamed mixture. Add the flour and baking powder and stir until the mixture starts to form a ball.
- Spray an 8" or 9" pie plate with cooking spray.
- Press mixture into the pie plate and flute the edges.
- Pour the prepared berries into the crust and bake in the preheated 375° oven for 45 minutes until the pie bubbles in the center.
- Just before serving, sprinkle with sifted powdered sugar.

Kathy Hannah

1950s, the Hannah/ Lamkin beach, Good Hart

Fresh Strawberry or Raspberry Pie

This is a Good Hart family favorite. The filling may be made ahead and kept refrigerated until berries are available.

1 pie shell, baked and cooled
1 quart fresh strawberries or raspberries
1 cup crushed fresh strawberries or raspberries
1 cup sugar
3 tablespoons cornstarch
2 tablespoons lemon juice, if using strawberries
A few drops of red food coloring
2 tablespoons butter
Whipped cream or ice cream

- Wash and hull the fresh berries and place points up in the pie shell.

- In a saucepan combine 1 cup crushed berries with sugar and cornstarch and cook until clear.

- Add the lemon juice for strawberries. Add a few drops of red food coloring and the butter. Stir until thickened.

- Cool, stir, and pour over the berries in the pie shell.

- Top with whipped cream or ice cream.

Sally Lamkin

Ella Petoskey received her degree from the Carlisle school, celebrated for the Native American Olympian Jim Thorpe. She played Minnehaha in the Hiawatha pageant at Round Lake. She taught and worked summers at the Lamkin Indian Art store.

Fresh Strawberry or Raspberry Gelatin Pie

I was born and raised here on West Townline Road and can't imagine living anywhere else. I cut this recipe out of the newspaper many years ago. It always turns out a nice pie.

9" graham cracker pie crust

FILLING:
1 quart fresh strawberries or raspberries
3 tablespoons strawberry or raspberry Jell-O
3/4 cup sugar
3 tablespoons cornstarch
1 cup water

- Wash, cull and cut the berries and place them in the pie shell.
- Mix the Jell-O, sugar, cornstarch and water together in a saucepan.
- Boil until thickened then cool 10 minutes.
- Pour over the berries and refrigerate until set.

Marie Ward

Joseph Okenotego Francis, Middle Village, recipient of the Carnegie Medal for bravery, November 8, 1908. He and Joe Kisigoginessi took a rowboat one and a half miles out in Lake Michigan in gale force winds and heavy breakers to rescue three men whose boat had lost engine power.

Oatmeal Peach Pie

**1 large can peaches, drained and quartered (or use
  fresh peaches)**
3/4 cup oatmeal
1/2 cup brown sugar
1/2 cup flour
1/3 cup butter

- Preheat oven to 350^0.
- Grease a pie pan and line with peach quarters.
- Mix the oatmeal, brown sugar, flour and butter together and place mixture on top of the peaches.
- Bake for 30 minutes.

Mabel Lewis
from Patty Lewis

Oatmeal Pie

4 eggs, lightly beaten
1½ cups sugar
1½ cups light corn syrup
1½ cups quick oatmeal
1 cup coconut
1 cup butter, room temperature
2 unbaked pie shells

- Preheat oven to 350⁰.
- Mix the eggs, sugar and corn syrup together.
- Add the oatmeal, coconut and butter.
- Pour into 2 unbaked prepared pie shells.
- Bake for 45 minutes or until an inserted knife comes out clean.

Anna Saddison

Middle Village, an early photo. After the sawmill was built in Cross Village in the latter half of the 1800s, there were over 50 Native American homes in Middle Village.

Pecan Tassies

MAKES 48

My grandchildren won't visit without the promise of tassies. They're a great mini dessert instead of a slice of pecan pie.

CRUST:
1 cup butter, softened
6 ounces cream cheese, softened
2 cups flour

FILLING:
1/2 cup butter, softened
1 cup sugar
1 egg, lightly beaten
1½ cups chopped pecans
1 cup chopped dates
1 tablespoon vanilla

Powdered sugar for topping

- Preheat oven to 350^0.

- In a large bowl, combine the 1 cup butter, cream cheese and flour. Mix until well blended.

- Divide the dough into 4 equal parts then separate each part into 12 balls, all the same size.

- Place the balls in the cups of 4 ungreased miniature muffin tins.

- Using your thumb and forefinger, press each ball into its cup, working the dough evenly up the sides to the rim.

- Cream the remaining 1/2 cup butter with the sugar and the rest of the ingredients and mix well. Divide the mixture among the unbaked shells, filling each completely.

- Bake in the preheated 350^0 oven for 30 – 40 minutes. Cool on racks before removing the tarts from the tins.

- Sprinkle with powdered sugar before serving.

Jane Cardinal

Annie's Butter Raisin Tarts

Unbaked tart shells

2 eggs, beaten well
1 cup brown sugar
1/2 cup butter, softened
1 cup golden raisins
1 teaspoon vanilla
1/4 – 1/2 teaspoon lemon juice

- Preheat oven to 375^0.

- Using your favorite pie crust recipe or my choice of rolled Pillsbury Pie Crust (found in the refrigerator section), cut circles for the tart shells. I use a drinking glass that cuts to the exact size to fit my tart pan making it very easy.

- Mix the beaten eggs, brown sugar, butter, raisins, vanilla and lemon juice together and fill the tart shells.

- Bake for 15 minutes.

Robert Smith
RFC Fire and Rescue Squad Board Member
and "Retired" Medical First Responder

The Best Oatmeal Cookies

MAKES 48 COOKIES
1 cup butter, softened
1/2 cup granulated sugar
1/2 cup packed brown sugar
1/4 teaspoon baking soda
1 teaspoon baking powder
1 teaspoon ground cinnamon
1/4 teaspoon ground nutmeg
1/2 teaspoon salt
2 eggs at room temperature
1 teaspoon vanilla
1¾ cups all-purpose flour
3 cups rolled oats
1 cup semi-sweet chocolate chips
1/2 cup coarsely chopped almonds, toasted
1/2 cup coarsely chopped dried fruit such as dried
    cherries

- Preheat oven to 375⁰.
- In a large mixing bowl beat the butter on medium speed for 1 minute. Add the sugars, baking soda, baking powder, cinnamon, nutmeg and salt. Beat until well combined.
- Beat in 1 egg at a time and then add the vanilla. Beat in the flour and then fold in the oats. You may need to finish adding the oats by hand.
- Fold in chocolate chips, toasted almonds and dried fruit.
- Drop by rounded teaspoons 2 inches apart on ungreased cookie sheets.
- Bake in the preheated 375⁰ oven for 8 – 10 minutes.
- Cool on a wire rack.

Mary Rapin
Bliss Gardens Farm & Community Kitchen

Photo by Patricia Clarke

Oatmeal "Cry Baby" Cookies

This was my Grandmother Good's recipe and it was waiting on a plate in our kitchen when I came home from school. It was one of my favorite cookies and I wish I'd asked why my grandmother called them "Cry Baby Cookies."

MAKES 24 -36 COOKIES depending on size
2 cups brown sugar
1 cup vegetable shortening
2 eggs
1 teaspoon vanilla
2 cups rolled oatmeal
1 cup sour milk (To make sour milk, add 1/2 teaspoon lemon juice to 1 cup milk.)
4 cups flour
1 teaspoon baking soda
A pinch of salt
1 cup raisins, optional

- Preheat oven to 375⁰.
- Cream the brown sugar, shortening and eggs together then add the vanilla.
- Soak the oatmeal in the sour milk.
- Mix all of the above together and stir in the flour, baking soda and salt.
- Fold in 1 cup of raisins if desired.
- Drop by the spoonful on ungreased cookie sheets.
- Bake for 10 – 12 minutes.

Connie Cobb

No Flour Peanut Butter Cookies

These are super easy and yummy.

1 cup peanut butter
1 cup sugar, white or brown
1 egg

- Preheat oven to 300^0.
- Mix all ingredients together.
- Spoon mixture onto an ungreased cookie sheet.
- Bake for 12 – 15 minutes.

Laura Ward

Aunt Sara's Ice Box Cookies

Aunt Sara's cookies were neat and pretty. Mine aren't. The first time I made them for the Junior Goodwill Country Store, I sent a note stating: "These cookies taste better than they look." They put the note up with the cookies and people came back for years asking for "those cookies that taste better than they look."

1/2 cup butter (Sara used shortening but I use butter or margarine.)
1/2 cup dark brown sugar, firmly packed
3/4 cup granulated sugar
1 egg, slightly beaten
1 teaspoon vanilla
2 cups flour
1/2 teaspoon salt
2 teaspoons baking powder
1/2 cup chopped pecans

- Mix butter, sugars, egg and vanilla together in a large bowl.

- Combine flour, salt and baking powder and add to the mixture.

- Fold in the nuts.

- Make rolls of the mixture. (Sara's were rectangular; mine end up round but it doesn't matter.)

- Chill the rolls until firm.

- Preheat oven to 400⁰.

- Slice the cookies very thinly.

- Place on greased cookie sheets and bake for 8 – 10 minutes depending on the thickness of the cookies.

Mary Beth Mellen

Joe Donatus and Helen Gablo pose for a postcard in Good Hart — note the type of arrow.

Very Best Gingerbread Men

4 cups flour
1 cup salt
2 teaspoons baking powder
1 teaspoon baking soda
2 teaspoons ground ginger
2 teaspoons ground cloves
3 teaspoons cinnamon
1 teaspoon nutmeg
1 cup vegetable shortening
2 cups sugar
2 egg yolks
1 cup dark molasses

ICING:
2 egg whites
3 – 3½ cups sifted powdered sugar
Food coloring, optional

- Sift flour, salt, baking powder, baking soda, ginger, cloves, cinnamon and nutmeg together.

- In a large bowl cream the shortening, sugar, egg yolks and molasses together.

- Gradually add the sifted dry ingredients.

- Cover and chill at least 1 hour.

- Preheat oven to 350^0.

- Divide dough into fourths. Roll out, 1 portion at a time, to 1/4-inch thickness.

- Cut with cookie cutters or form into creations then place on ungreased cookie sheets.

- Bake 5 – 8 minutes in the preheated 350^0 oven.

- Make decorative icing by beating the 2 egg whites until frothy then gradually beating in the sifted powdered sugar. Add food coloring if desired.

- When the cookies are cool, decorate with icing as desired.

Kathy Hannah

This recipe started out as "Gingerbread Men" but in the summers of the 1970s it became an art form in the guise of the Annual Good Hart Gingerbread Bake. The kids used rolling pins and cookie cutters but also formed the dough like clay into all kinds of creations. The dough can be handled a lot without becoming tough. The kids learned that tall masterpieces wouldn't work as they "puddled" when baked, but many other masterpieces were, indeed, created. The evening of the event, the parents came to the art exhibit and the artists described their gingerbread art. Then everyone got to eat and enjoy! In the summer of 2008, we reinstituted the Annual Gingerbread Bake and invited the children of the original artists. It was so much fun that we'll keep it going.

Living in Good Hart

Dorothy Mange spent summers with her brothers and mother at their cottage on the shore in Chippewa Cove. The Bliss children were their playmates. In 1939 Dorothy married Monnie Bliss and eventually they built their home on Lake Shore Drive. Although Dorothy grew up near Grand Rapids, she learned to love northern Michigan, especially walks in the woods and on the lake shore. Piano music was the love of her life and she taught piano to many area children and played piano and organ in area churches.

Christmas Cut-Out Cookies

This recipe was a Bliss family favorite. Dorothy supplied freshly decorated cookies for her children and their friends. The children looked forward to these holiday cookies after a long school bus ride from Harbor Springs to Good Hart.

2 cups shortening
3 cups sugar
4 eggs
1/4 cup milk
4 teaspoons vanilla
5 cups flour
1 teaspoon baking powder
1 teaspoon salt
Decorative sugars

- Preheat oven to 350⁰.
- Mix all ingredients except decorative sugars together. The mixture will be thick. Chill.
- Roll and cut out with decorative cookie cutters.
- Decorate with sugars and place on greased cookie sheets.
- Bake in the preheated 350⁰ oven for 7 – 8 minutes.

Dorothy Bliss
via Bonnie Weitzel

Dorothy and Monnie Bliss at Blisswood

A Celebrity Chef offering . . . Kathy Smolak

Kolaczky (Traditional Polish Christmas and Easter Cookies)

We have lots of fun making these with grandkids.

1/2 cup butter, softened
1 3-ounce package cream cheese, softened
1¼ cups all-purpose flour
1/4 cup jam (apricot, raspberry, strawberry or prune)
1/4 cup confectioners' sugar

Stan Smolak, creator of Legs Inn and its fantastic décor

- Beat the butter and cream cheese together in a bowl until light and fluffy.

- Gradually add the flour and mix until combined.

- Wrap the dough in plastic wrap and chill in the refrigerator for 30 minutes.

- Preheat oven to 375^0.

- Roll out the dough to 1/8 inch thickness on a floured surface.

- Cut into 2-inch circles with a cookie cutter or glass.

- Spoon 1/4 teaspoon of jam into the center of each circle.

- Fold opposite edges together.

- Place approximately 2 inches apart on greased cookie sheets.

- Bake in the preheated 375^0 oven for approximately 15 minutes.

- Sprinkle with confectioners' sugar.

Smacznego!

Kathy Smolak
Legs Inn

Great Grandma's Soft Molasses Cookies

1 cup melted shortening, cooled
1 cup brown sugar
1 cup molasses
1 teaspoon vinegar
1 egg, beaten
3½ – 4 cups flour
2 teaspoons baking soda
1 teaspoon cinnamon
Pinch salt
1 cup sour cream
Raspberry jam, optional

- Preheat oven to 375°.
- Mix shortening, brown sugar, molasses, vinegar and egg in a large mixing bowl.
- Combine flour, baking soda, cinnamon and salt and add alternately with sour cream to the shortening mixture.
- Drop by the spoonful onto an ungreased cookie sheet.
- Slightly flatten and add a dab of raspberry jam to the top if desired.
- Bake for 10 – 12 minutes.

Adina Foster
via Georgie Richner

Adina Foster at the Good Hart Store and Post Office

Scotch Shortbread

1 cup butter, softened
2/3 cup sugar
2⅔ cups flour, sifted

- Preheat oven to 350^0.
- Cream butter and sugar until light and fluffy.
- Add the flour slowly and beat until crumbly.
- Spread on a small cookie sheet with sides (about 9" x 13"). Press down to 1/4-inch thickness. Prick with a fork and bake for 20 minutes.
- Cut into 18 squares while hot.

Ann Churchill

A Churchill family cottage – this squared timber pioneer antique now resides along the Tunnel of Trees.

Crazy Chocolate Cookies

Kids love making and eating these.

1 stack saltine crackers
1 cup sugar
1 cup butter
1 12-ounce package semi-sweet chocolate chips
1 cup chopped nuts
Decorative sprinkles, optional

- Preheat oven to 350^0.
- Line a jelly roll pan with foil. Cover the bottom of the pan with a single layer of crackers.
- Combine the butter and sugar in a saucepan and boil for 3 minutes.
- Drizzle over the crackers being sure to cover all.
- Bake in the preheated 350^0 oven for 15 minutes.
- Remove from oven and sprinkle with chocolate chips.
- When the chocolate melts, smooth over all and add the nuts. You may add decorative sprinkles if desired. Refrigerate.
- When cold, break into pieces.

Marge Edwards

Chocolate Pleasers

2 cups Crispix cereal
3/4 cup chopped cocktail peanuts
1 cup butterscotch morsels
1/2 cup semi-sweet chocolate morsels

- In a large bowl, combine the cereal and peanuts; set aside.

- Place butterscotch and chocolate morsels in a small microwave-safe bowl. Heat on high for 2 minutes, stirring after 1 minute. Stir morsels until smooth.

- Pour melted morsels over the cereal and peanuts. Stir until well coated.

- Drop by round teaspoons onto a cookie sheet. Chill until firm.

- Refrigerate in an airtight container.

Donna Wood

SHORE DRIVE   HARBOR SPRINGS, MICHIGAN.

Whirligigs

Bill and Esther Freeman knew every bird along North Lake Shore Drive by name. They had more bird feeders than any catalog could boast and they cared for every feathered friend that called Good Hart home. Esther made these delicious cookies for human friends.

1/2 cup peanut butter
1/2 cup shortening
1/2 cup granulated sugar
1/2 cup brown sugar
1 egg
1¼ cups flour
1/2 teaspoon baking soda
1/2 teaspoon salt
1 generous cup chocolate chips

- Preheat oven to 375⁰.
- Cream the peanut butter, shortening and sugars together thoroughly.
- Add the egg and beat until light and fluffy.
- Mix the flour, baking soda and salt and add to the egg mixture.
- Roll the dough into a rectangle1/4 inch thick.
- Melt the chips in a saucepan over hot but not boiling water.
- Cool the chocolate slightly and spread on the dough. Starting on the long side, roll the dough like a jelly roll and slice into 1/4 inch slices.
- Place on ungreased cookie sheets and bake in the preheated 375⁰ oven for 10 – 12 minutes.

Esther Freeman
via Carolyn Sutherland

Biz Bauer Wallick's Version of Seven-Layer Cookies

1 stick butter, melted
1 cup graham cracker crumbs
1 12-ounce package semi-sweet chocolate chips
1 10-ounce package peanut butter chips
1 tablespoon coconut
1 14-ounce can sweetened condensed milk
1½ cups chopped walnuts or pecans

- Preheat oven to 350^0.
- Put melted butter in a 9" x 13" pan.
- Add the graham cracker crumbs then each of the other ingredients in the order listed.
- Bake for 20 minutes.
- Allow time to set up then cut into bars. If they don't set up as bars, pop them in the freezer for 30 minutes and you are good to go.

Biz Bauer Wallick

Homesteader Winter Apples

Families in Good Hart sent their children to school with dry apple pie in their winter lunch buckets. To dry apples, peel, core and cut 32-36 apples in eighths. Place the slices so they do not touch each other on cookie sheets in a $110\text{-}150^0$ oven for six hours, turning twice. They should be dry outside and soft inside; there should be no moisture when squeezed. Place in a loosely covered container and mix several times a day for five days before storing in paper covered jars.

Indian pipes

Chocolate Pecan Squares

CRUST:
1¼ pounds unsalted butter at room temperature
3/4 cup granulated sugar
3 extra-large eggs
3/4 teaspoon vanilla
4½ cups all-purpose flour
1/2 teaspoon baking powder
1/4 teaspoon salt

TOPPING:
1 pound unsalted butter
1 cup good honey
3 cups light brown sugar, packed
1 teaspoon grated lemon zest
1 teaspoon grated orange zest
1/4 cup heavy cream
2 pounds pecans, coarsely chopped
12 ounces milk chocolate, melted in a double boiler

- Preheat oven to 350^0.

- For the crust, beat the butter and granulated sugar with an electric mixer until light and fluffy, approximately 3 minutes. Add the eggs and vanilla and mix well.

- Sift the flour, baking powder and salt. Mix the dry ingredients into the batter with the mixer on low speed until just combined.

- Press the dough evenly into an ungreased 18" x 12" x 1" baking sheet, making an edge around the outside. It will be sticky so sprinkle the dough and your hands with flour before pressing. Prick the crust with a fork.
- Bake in the preheated 350^0 oven for 15 minutes until the crust is set but not browned.
- Allow to cool.
- For the topping, combine the butter, honey, brown sugar and zests in a large, heavy bottom saucepan. Cook over low heat until the butter melts using a wooden spoon to stir. Raise the heat and boil for 3 minutes. Remove from the heat and stir in the heavy cream and pecans.
- Pour mixture over the crust. As the filling will bubble over the edge, place a larger baking sheet on a lower level rack to catch the drips.
- Bake in the preheated 350^0 oven for 25 – 30 minutes until the filling is set.
- Remove from the oven and cool.
- Wrap in plastic wrap and refrigerate until cold. Cut into squares and dip half of each square in the melted chocolate.

Lindsey Pfaff
Former RFC First Responder

Paul's Pumpkin Bars

BARS:
2 cups all-purpose flour
2 teaspoons baking powder
2 teaspoons cinnamon
1 teaspoon baking soda
1/4 teaspoon salt
4 eggs
1 15-ounce can pumpkin
1⅔ cups sugar
1 cup canola oil
3/4 cup chopped pecans, optional

FROSTING:
1 3-ounce package cream cheese, softened
1/4 cup butter, softened
1 teaspoon vanilla
2 cups sifted confectioners' sugar

Additional pecan halves if desired for garnish

- Preheat oven to 350^0.
- In a medium bowl, stir together the flour, baking powder, cinnamon, baking soda and salt. Set aside.
- In a large bowl, beat the eggs, pumpkin, sugar and oil together. Add flour mixture and beat until well combined.
- Fold in the chopped pecans if desired.
- Spread the batter in an ungreased 15" x 10" x 1" baking pan.
- Bake for 25 – 30 minutes or until a toothpick comes out clean.
- Cool on a wire rack.
- To make the frosting combine the cream cheese, butter, vanilla and confectioners' sugar and beat until smooth. Spread frosting on cooled bars and top with additional pecan halves if desired.
- Store in the refrigerator.

Christine Bommarito

CARDINAL

Blondies

These are dedicated to Emily, the blonde in our family.

1 stick butter or margarine
1 cup brown sugar
1 egg
1 teaspoon vanilla
1 cup flour
1/2 teaspoon salt
1 cup semi-sweet chocolate chips

- Preheat oven to 350^0.
- Melt the butter and then add the sugar and stir until smooth.
- Transfer to a large bowl and beat 1 minute. Add egg and vanilla and beat until light and fluffy.
- Stir in the flour and salt and then fold in the chocolate chips. Spread in a greased and floured 8" square pan.
- Bake for 20 – 25 minutes. Do not overbake!
- Cool completely, and then cut into squares.

Susan Richner

Betty's Brownies

1/2 cup butter, softened
2 cups sugar
4 eggs
4 squares baking chocolate, melted
1 teaspoon vanilla
1 cup flour
1 cup chopped walnuts

- Preheat oven to 325⁰.
- Cream the butter and sugar together then add the remaining ingredients and mix until combined.
- Spread brownie mixture into a greased 9" x 13" pan lined with wax paper.
- Bake for 35 minutes or until a toothpick inserted in the center comes out clean.
- Slightly cool then invert the pan and peel off the wax paper.
- Cut into squares.

Sally Kelsey

1950s. Sally's sister Mary fishes off the remains of the Cross Village dock from the Lumbering era.

Cross Village Generations

We live year round in Cross Village and I'm the fourth generation of the Andrew and Susie Kruskie family. My mother, Ethel Kruskie Lawler, still lives in the area. We enjoy being a part of Holy Cross Church, the Harbor Springs Outdoor Club and the Snowmobile Club.

Cross Village, Coleen's great grandmother, Elizabeth Ransom (Williams), 26, holds great aunt Ida as her grandmother Susie, then two years, stands at the left.

Bread Pudding with Whiskey Sauce

PUDDING:
1 loaf day-old (dry) French bread, torn or cubed
1 quart milk
3 eggs
2 cups sugar
3 tablespoons vanilla
1 cup raisins
3 tablespoons butter or margarine

SAUCE:
1 stick (8 tablespoons) butter or margarine, softened
1 cup sugar
1 egg, beaten
Whiskey to taste

- Preheat oven to 325°.

- Soak the bread in the milk. Crush with hands until well mixed. Add eggs, sugar, vanilla and raisins and stir well.

- Melt the 3 tablespoons butter or margarine and pour in the bottom of a thick 9" x 13" pan. Spread the bread, egg, sugar, vanilla and raisin mixture over the melted butter. Bake until very firm, approximately 75 minutes.

- Let cool and cube the pudding and put into individual ramekins or oven-safe dessert dishes.

- To make the sauce, cream the butter and sugar. Cook in a double boiler until very hot and sugar is well dissolved. Add the well-beaten egg and whip quickly so the egg doesn't curdle.

- Let cool and add whiskey to taste.

- When ready to serve, pour the sauce over the bread pudding and heat under the broiler.

Coleen McClive

Holy Cross Church in Cross Village

On the arched stained glass window above the entrance to Holy Cross Church is the date 1691 when history records that Jesuit missionaries erected the cross on the Lake Michigan shore from which Cross Village would take its name. Also depicted is the first wigwam mission church called Anamiewatigoing, "prayer place near the cross."

In the 1700s, Odawa master carpenter Joseh Ainse built a log church on the bluff. Throughout Cross Village's 300-year history, Catholic priests, brothers and sisters ministered to, taught, and baptized hundreds of Odawa families and later the settlers who arrived in the late 1800s.

Prominent priests included Bishop Frederic Baraga who arrived in 1831. He learned the Odawa language from William Blackbird. For 40 years, Baraga traveled and labored extensively throughout the region. His devotion to the Native Americans endeared him to those he served. During his tenure, in 1850, the Cross Village Indian Cemetery was consecrated.

In 1855, eccentric Father Bernard Weikamp, a Prussian, arrived in Cross Village. During the next 35 years, he built a large convent, a parochial school and a second church. Today, the school serves as the Cross Village Township Hall.

In 1895, the Franciscans began to minister in Cross Village and a new church was planned. Its altar, from a church on Mackinac Island, was hauled by horses and sled over the straits in the winter of 1895-96. Two years later, the new church called Holy Cross was dedicated. It is also commemorated in the stained glass window welcoming worshipers to Holy Cross.

The Franciscan church, Holy Cross, with the sisters' house on the left

The school yard

Apple Betty

This is my son's favorite dessert and it's much easier to make than pie.

MAKES 6 SERVINGS
5 – 6 cups sliced apples
1 teaspoon cinnamon
1/4 cup water
1/3 cup cold butter
3/4 cup flour
1 cup sugar

- Preheat oven to 350^0.
- Butter a 10" x 6" x 2" casserole dish.
- Mix apples, cinnamon and water and pour into the casserole dish.
- Cut the butter into the flour and sugar.
- Spread crumbles of the mixture over the apples.
- Bake for 40 minutes.
- Serve warm with whipped cream or ice cream.

Holly Hillier

Individual Peach Crisps

Peaches (use half a peach per serving)
1 tablespoon brown sugar per peach half
2 tablespoons granola per peach half
1 pat of butter per peach half

- Preheat oven to 400⁰.
- Cut peaches in half and place in a baking dish, removing the pits.
- Into each peach place 1 tablespoon brown sugar and 2 tablespoons granola.
- Top each with a pat of butter. (I forgot the butter once and they were still good.)
- Bake for 20 minutes.
- Serve with vanilla ice cream.

Pam O'Malley

REV. J. B. WEIKAMP.

Cross Village. It is said that Father Weikamp prayed daily in his mausoleum and it was reported that he was seen there in prayer after his death. This tidbit of village lore gave rise to lots of childhood pranks around Halloween.

Frozen Lemon-Ginger Yogurt or Ice Cream

This is one that Ben and Jerry haven't thought of yet.

1/2 gallon vanilla frozen yogurt or ice cream, softened
1/4 cup honey
2 tablespoons lemon juice
1 tablespoon fresh ginger, peeled and minced
2 teaspoons lemon peel, grated
1/4 teaspoon ground ginger (or more if desired)

- Mix honey, lemon juice, minced ginger, grated lemon peel and ground ginger together.
- Add the mixture to the softened ice cream
- Refreeze.

Maureen Mayne

1950s. The Grove Shop featured Native American baskets and crafts north of Good Hart on the Tunnel of Trees.

Rice Pudding Custard

My grandmother, Edith Lughbil, made this for me as an after school treat when I was six years old. Later, when I was eight or so she would let me help her make it up and bake it. It's one of my favorite dishes.

1 cup cooked rice, dry and fluffy
2 cups milk
3/4 cup sugar
1/4 teaspoon salt
3 eggs, beaten
1 teaspoon vanilla
1/2 cup raisins
Dash nutmeg over the top

- Preheat oven to 350^0.
- Mix all ingredients together except nutmeg.
- Pour into a buttered baking dish.
- Bake for 45-60 minutes.
- Sprinkle top with nutmeg.

Dianna Hoffman

Strawberry-Pretzel Jell-O Dessert

2 cups crushed pretzels
3/4 cup melted butter or margarine
3 tablespoons sugar
1 8-ounce package cream cheese, softened
1 cup sugar
1 9-ounce container Cool Whip non-dairy topping, thawed
1 6-ounce box strawberry Jell-O
2 cups boiling water
2 4-ounce packages frozen strawberries

- Mix the crushed pretzels, melted butter and 3 tablespoons sugar together and press into a 9" x 13" pan.
- Cream the cream cheese and 1 cup sugar together then add the non-dairy topping. Spread over the pretzels.
- Mix the strawberry Jell-O, boiling water and strawberries and let stand for 10 minutes then pour over the mixture in the pan.
- Refrigerate until set.

Anna Saddison

A Celebrity Chef offering . . . Nancy Kelly

Pellston Market's Delice de Chocolat

MAKES 6
200 grams imported bittersweet chocolate
3 eggs
1/3 cup sugar
1 cup whipping cream

- Finely chop the chocolate and melt slowly in a mixing bowl set over simmering water. (Do not cover or splash water into the chocolate as it could cause it to become granular.)

- Combine eggs and sugar in a standing mixer and beat for 13 minutes. The mixture will triple in volume and become light and fluffy.

- Pour or scrape the melted chocolate into the beaten egg mixture and blend with the mixer.

- In a clean, chilled bowl, beat the whipping cream to near the stiff peak stage. (You should be able to take out the mixer and have the top of the peaks just falling over; if it is too stiff it will not blend into the chocolate smoothly.)

- Whisk 1/4 of the cream into the chocolate mixture to lighten it. Then, with a spatula, gently fold the rest of the cream into the lightened chocolate.

- Pour into small bowls or ramekins and refrigerate until set.

- It will be decadent and delicious!

Chef Nancy Kelly
Pellston Market

Nancy Kelly

Maple Sugar

An Historic Native American Food

March signals the beginning of maple sugaring. Warm sunny days and crisp frigid nights bring the best sap harvest. In the mid-1800s, Bishop Baraga, the missionary, wrote about the Michigan Native American sugar camps. Their production astounded him. He noted that the average Ottawa family produced two thousand pounds of sugar. This is all the more remarkable as it takes seven or eight gallons of sap to produce one pound of sugar.

Processing the sugar was a 24-hour-a-day operation during which the family stayed in a portion of the sugar longhouse. With little time for anything else, families lived mostly on sugar and maple syrup for three months.

They produced four types of sugar products. Grain sugar (cassonade in French) was stored while still warm in birch bark makaks that weighed up to 80 pounds. Syrup, not as easily stored, was consumed quickly. To preserve some syrup for table use, pioneer families cooked up a very thick syrup to keep it from souring. They then sealed it in jugs that they buried two to three feet deep where it kept for a year.

Native Americans and pioneers both made maple syrup cakes. They carved molds into five to six-inch basswood boards. Depending on the carver's skill, the molds were made in simple shapes including rabbits, bears, leaves or stars or whatever the family chose. Just before crystallization, hot, thick syrup was poured into these molds. Native Americans used these molded candies as gifts.

Sugar gum or wax was a child's delight. When the cooked syrup reached a proper consistency, birch bark "casseaus" (deep tray-like containers) were filled with fresh snow. The syrup was then thrown over the snow where it hardened into sugar taffy. Whatever wasn't eaten at the time was stored between thin sheets of birch bark tied with bast, a cord made from bark lining cut into thin strips.

Maple Sugar Popcorn Balls

1/4 cup popping corn
1 cup maple syrup
1⅓ teaspoons butter
1/2 teaspoon salt, optional

- Pop and sort the popped corn, discarding the "old maids," kernels that haven't popped.

- Place the popped corn in a heat-proof bowl.

- Combine syrup and butter with salt if desired in a heavy saucepan and cook over medium-high heat, stirring constantly. When a candy thermometer reaches 250^0, put a few drops of the candy into cold water. It should form soft balls.

- When ready, pour the candy over the popped corn. When the mixture is cool enough to handle, butter your hands and form the popcorn into balls.

- Cool on a buttered surface and store in an airtight container.

Jane Cardinal

Maple Sap Tonic

In the spring, woodsmen and farmers tapped maple trees and used the sap as a drink in place of water. The liquid had just enough sugar and maple flavor to make it a delicious and satisfying drink. The sap was thought to have medicinal virtue...a sort of spring tonic like sulphur and molasses.

Over the years the Good Hart Indian Art Store of the Lamkin family changed identity with subsequent owners (see Bread, Breakfast and Brunch pg. 44). Charlotte Burton's shop was the earliest. Currently this heritage gift shop is known as A Studio.

Ghirardelli Truffles

MAKES ABOUT 30 TRUFFLES
1/4 cup heavy whipping cream
2 4-ounce bars Ghirardelli Bittersweet Chocolate, broken into 1/4 inch pieces
6 tablespoons unsalted butter, cut into small pieces
1/3 cup unsweetened cocoa

- In a small saucepan bring the cream to a simmer. Remove from heat and stir in the chocolate and the butter.
- In a medium skillet bring half an inch of water to a simmer. Set the saucepan in the skillet over low heat and stir until the chocolate has melted.
- Remove from heat and pour into a shallow bowl. Cover and refrigerate for at least 2 hours.
- Pour the cocoa into a pie plate.
- Line an air-tight container with wax paper.
- Tip a melon baller or teaspoon into a glass of warm water then quickly pull across the chilled chocolate mixture to form a rough 1-inch ball.
- Drop the ball into the cocoa and roll it around to coat. Place in the wax paper-lined tin, separating the layers with wax paper. Cover tightly and refrigerate up to 2 weeks or freeze up to 3 months.

Ann Churchill

Super Easy Fudge

**1 14-ounce can sweetened condensed milk (Don't use
evaporated milk.)**
1 12-ounce package semi-sweet chocolate chips
Pinch of salt
1½ teaspoons vanilla
1½ cups chopped nuts, optional

- Cook the sweetened condensed milk, chocolate chips
  and salt together in a saucepan over medium heat.
  When the chocolate has melted stir in the vanilla and
  the chopped nuts.

- Line an 8" x 8" pan with wax paper. Pour the fudge in
  the pan and chill.

- Cut when cool.

- To double the recipe, use a 9" x 13" pan.

Wortley Family

Heritage Recipes . . .

Chocolate Sundae Sauce

4 squares unsweetened chocolate
1 cup water
1 cup light corn syrup
1 cup dark corn syrup
1 cup sugar
1 teaspoon salt
1 teaspoon vanilla

- Melt the chocolate, water, light and dark corn syrup, sugar and salt in a saucepan.
- Simmer 10 minutes stirring constantly.
- Remove from heat and add the vanilla.

Ruby Wyland
Hemlock House

Peanut Butter Sundae Sauce

Ruby is gone as is the Hemlock House, but many have fond memories of her wonderful just plain good food.

1 cup sugar
1/2 cup water
2/3 cup light corn syrup
1/2 teaspoon salt
1/4 cup peanut butter

- Combine the sugar, water, light corn syrup and salt in a saucepan.
- Bring to a boil and cook over low heat for 2 minutes.
- Cool to room temperature.
- Add the peanut butter and blend until smooth.

Ruby Wyland
Hemlock House

Canning & Preserving

Leaning Trees at Middle Village Beach, 1950s, by Virgil D. Haynes
©Haynes Studio, Harbor Springs

CARDINAL

Recipes

Home Canning

Many of today's food preservation and canning safety procedures have changed from the ones our parents and grandparents used, and so we encourage you to review recent and updated methods.

The *National Center for Home Food Preservation* is one definitive standard for home food canning and preserving procedures provided by the United States Department of Agriculture (USDA). The center's information is available at the University of Georgia Cooperative Extension website: www.UGA.edu/NCHFP

Another user-friendly source for home canners comes from an old standby — *Better Homes and Gardens* magazine. Their website — www.BHG.com/yesyoucan — sparkles with how-to tips for choosing the right equipment, and easy-to-understand guidelines and instructions, not to mention delicious recipes.

All the recipes in this Home Canning section assume that cooks will use sterile jars and lids. The canning jars you use should be filled to within 1/4 inch to 1/2 inch of the top or the jars won't seal correctly. And most recipes require a hot water bath after jars are sealed. Again, please check the website above for the most recent canning safety instructions.

Long ago, preserving food with an "expert" at your elbow led many families to keep their home canning traditions alive. Perhaps your family will find a new tradition among the favorites that follow.

Dilly Beans

These are great to have on hand as an instant appetizer. I have served them plain (just drained and presented in a pretty, oblong dish), or as an hors d'oeuvre with a crosswise slice of Dilly Bean on a piece of white cheddar atop a cracker of choice.

PER WIDE-MOUTH PINT JAR:
Green beans (Calculate the number of green beans needed to fill the number of wide-mouth pint jars you have.)
1/4 teaspoon cayenne pepper
1 clove garlic, peeled and cut in half
Sprig of fresh dill

- Wash and trim green beans and sort into similar sizes.

BRINE:
1 gallon water
1 gallon white vinegar
1¾ cups salt

- In a large stock pot, mix the brine together, bring to a boil and keep hot.

- Sterilize jars. To each jar add the cayenne pepper, garlic and dill sprigs.

- Place beans vertically into each jar.

- Pour hot brine into each jar and fill to within 1/4 inch from the top.

- Screw on lids and bands and process 10 minutes in boiling water bath.

Kathy Hannah

The Hemlock Central heads for a Harbor Springs lumber mill through pioneer farm lands.

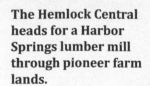

Pam's Bread & Butter Pickles

MAKES 14 pints
Pickle mixture:
1 peck cucumbers, sliced
26 small onions, chopped
4 green peppers, chopped
6 red peppers, chopped
2 cups coarse salt

- Sprinkle mixture with the 2 cups of salt.
- Let stand overnight.
- In the morning, rinse with clear water. Drain thoroughly.

SYRUP:
2 quarts cider vinegar
9 cups granulated sugar
1/4 cup mustard seeds
1 tablespoon plus 1½ teaspoons celery seeds
3 teaspoons turmeric

- In large pot, combine syrup ingredients. Add pickle mixture. Heat thoroughly and slowly bring to boiling point, but don't boil.
- Put in jars, seal and process in hot water bath.

Karen DeMars Pillsbury

A Celebrity Chef offering . . . Sharon Spencer

Pond Hill Farm Dilly Beans

Pond Hill Farm ...

This family-focused destination for locals and visitors alike is situated on a big bend along the Tunnel of Trees near Five Mile Creek. A dirt drive leads to the panorama of Pond Hill's farmland, greenhouses, barn, pastures and country market and café.

In 1980, the Spencer family came from Chicago to Harbor Springs to live the country life. They purchased 73 acres of land, adding another 80 a few years later. Their site had swamp, hills, fields, woods, a stream and best of all, a place for a pond. Almost immediately, Jim and Sharon Spencer and their children started digging a pond, and that's how Pond Hill Farm got its name.

Along with the pond came dogs, ducks, chickens, turkeys, geese, sheep, goats and Black Angus cows. Their first farm "store" set up in 1994 was a large wooden crate with fresh eggs and an Honest Box set up at the end of the driveway.

Continued next page

PER QUART JAR:
Green beans, standing on end very tightly packed in a 1-quart jar
1 hot chili pepper
1 clove garlic
Fresh dill
Grape leaf

BRINE:
3 cups white vinegar
6 tablespoons salt
3/4 teaspoon cayenne pepper
6 cloves garlic, minced
9 cups water

- Sterilize jars.
- Mix brine ingredients in large pot and bring to a boil.
- Into each sterilized quart jar put 1 dry hot chili pepper, 1 garlic "toe" (clove), fresh dill and grape leaf.
- Fill jar with green beans stood on end very tightly.
- Pour boiling brine over the beans to 1/2 inch of top.
- Secure lids and process for 10 minutes in boiling water bath.

Sharon Spencer
Pond Hill Farm

A Celebrity Chef offering . . . Sharon Spencer

Pond Hill Farm Bread & Butter Pickles

PICKLES:
4 quarts cucumbers, sliced
8 medium onions, peeled and sliced
2 heaping tablespoons salt

- Mix together and add 1 quart cold water.
- Let stand 2 hours. Drain.

BRINE:
3 cups vinegar
1 cup water
3 cups sugar
1 teaspoon turmeric
1 tablespoon celery seed
1 tablespoon mustard seeds

- Sterilize jars.
- Bring brine to a boil.
- Add drained cucumbers and onion.
- Bring to a boil again.
- Put in jars and process for 10 minutes in a boiling water bath.

Sharon Spencer
Pond Hill Farm

Soon, greenhouses and a livestock barn were built. In recent years honey bees, asparagus, u-pick strawberries and raspberries, a vineyard, hay rides, nature walks, three ponds and a canning kitchen have been added, along with Bess, the mama pig whose 15 piglets have delighted visitors.

And the pond that was dug those many years ago? Today, it's stocked with rainbow trout and bass and open for fishing through a catch and release program.

For the Spencers, "Farming is a way of life and a responsibility to yourself, your land, animals and your neighbors." Each season finds Pond Hill busy making maple syrup, gathering fresh produce, cut flowers, harvesting winter squash and pumpkins, and creating natural holiday wreaths and garlands, fresh soaps, and gift baskets filled with farm-canned crops.

A Celebrity Chef offering . . . Sharon Spencer

Pond Hill Dill Pickles

PER QUART JAR:
Small cucumbers
Fresh dill sprigs
4 black peppercorns
2 dried red chili peppers
1 clove garlic, peeled

- Into each quart jar, place the cucumbers, dill sprigs to taste, black peppercorns, red chili peppers and garlic.

BRINE:
2¾ cups white vinegar
3 cups water
1/4 cup salt

- Bring brine to boiling. Pour into jar filled with small cucumbers to 1/2 inch of top.
- Process for 10 minutes in boiling water bath.

Sharon Spencer
Pond Hill Farm

Sharon Spencer

Refrigerator Bread & Butter Pickles

These pickles are so easy because they are not exactly "canned." In our grandparent's day, food was preserved in crocks for the whole winter, not unlike these pickles which will keep in the refrigerator for a year or more. Just slice the cukes, pour the hot brine over them and put in the refrigerator when they've cooled. After three days they are ready to eat.

PICKLES:

14-15 small pickling cucumbers

- Wash and slice cucumbers and put them in a sterilized gallon jar.

BRINE:

4½ cups vinegar

4½ cups sugar

3/4 cup salt

1½ teaspoons turmeric

1½ teaspoons celery seed

Dill, about 4 heads

Garlic, about 3 buds (cloves)

- Mix all brine ingredients and bring to a boil.
- Pour over sliced cucumbers, dill and garlic in gallon jar.
- Store in the refrigerator and they are ready to eat in 3 days.

Louise Moser
via Rosie Stolt

Three-Day Dills

MAKES 3 QUARTS

The unusual thing about these pickles is that they are ready to eat in three days. Before canning, you may cut these pickles in quarters and put them in a wide-mouth pint jar; then they are ready to use when opened.

Small fresh cucumbers, about a peck
1/2 tablespoon mustard seed (1½ teaspoon)
1/4 teaspoon alum
1 large clove garlic or more
Dill, a good amount, to taste

- Scrub and clean cucumbers. Place in sterilized quart (or pint) jars.

- Into each jar put the seasonings. Halve the seasonings if using pint jars.

BRINE for 3 quarts of pickles:
3 cups apple cider vinegar
3 cups water
5 tablespoons kosher salt

- Boil brine.

- Cover the cucumbers with hot brine.

- Process in a hot water bath for 5 minutes (no longer or the pickles will not be crisp).

- These dills can be eaten after 3 days.

Mary Pifer
via Rosie Stolt

Icicle Pickles

This heritage recipe circa 1910 is copied as it was originally written.

2 gallon small pickles, split lengthwise or crosswise.
1 pint salt with boiling water to cover pickles.

- Let stand 1 week. Stir every morning.
- Drain. Cover with boiling water and leave 24 hours.

Alum, size of walnut

- Dissolve in water and mix into water on pickles.
- Let stand 24 hours more.
- Drain.

2½ quarts white vinegar
8 pints sugar
Mixed spices, large handful

- Boil together and pour over pickles, canning on the fourth morning.
- Seal while hot.

Leona Wyland Johnston

The interior of the Hemlock House Restaurant. Leona and Ruby, (pictured below), owned and cooked for this local treasure. Locals still get wistful over the oven-fresh breakfast cinnamon rolls they served.

Bobbie's Chili Sauce

MAKES 8 PINTS
30 medium size tomatoes (Roma preferred)
15-20 hot peppers (or banana peppers)
1/2 bunch celery
4 large onions
4 teaspoons salt
4 teaspoons each cloves, cinnamon and allspice
4 cups sugar
2 cups white vinegar

- Sterilize jars.
- Scald and peel tomatoes.
- Chop peppers, celery and onions.
- Add spices, sugar and vinegar.
- Cook uncovered on low heat until mixture thickens, several hours, stirring frequently.
- You can use the boiling water bath method.
- If the recipe is tripled, use 5 pounds of sugar and 1 quart vinegar.

Barbara Shirey
via Patricia Clarke

Harbor Springs. A gathering at Holy Childhood Church. On the right is the Globe Hotel later purchased by the church to house the teaching sisters of Notre Dame.

Cora's Chili Sauce

MAKES 4 PINTS

This is my mother-in-law's family-favorite chili sauce. She preferred older "under the counter" tomatoes because they were juicier. Her "dessert spoon" is a scant teaspoon. Whenever we canned together we would also enjoy a tomato and egg salad sandwich for lunch and I would listen happily to all her old family stories. Those were precious days.

18 ripe tomatoes (Remove skins by dropping in hot water and pulling off skins.)
6 medium onions, large dice (Put into the pot raw.)
1/2 teaspoon cayenne pepper
1 cup cider vinegar
1 teaspoon salt
1½ cups brown sugar

Cheesecloth bundle: (Put spices in the center of a 2-inch square of cheesecloth and tie with string.)
1 dessert spoon of cinnamon
1 dessert spoon of nutmeg
1 teaspoon celery seed
1 teaspoon whole cloves

- Crush tomatoes in a large pot.
- Add all ingredients including cheesecloth bundle; bring to a boil, lower heat and simmer uncovered for 3 hours, stirring frequently.
- Pack in sterile jars and process in a boiling water bath.

Carolyn Shear

Chippewa Woman Making a Birch Canoe

"As a matter of fact the whole family usually engage themselves in the making of the family canoe. The old men bring the stones with which the bark is weighted and the ribs kept in position; the younger men and boys collect the tamarack and cedar branches which are fashioned into ribs and gunwales, while the girls and squaws gather the pitch which will be used in closing the seams and the fibrous reeds which will sew together the various pieces of bark. It takes from one to two weeks of fairly constant labor to complete."

Stewed Tomatoes

MAKES 15-17 QUARTS

Use these tasty tomatoes in chili, spaghetti sauce and
    Spanish rice dishes.

1 bushel tomatoes, peeled and cored
1½ bunches celery, small dice
5 onions, small dice
4-5 green peppers, medium dice
1 heaping tablespoon coarse black pepper
1/2 cup kosher salt or more to taste

- Sterilize jars.
- Put all ingredients in a large pot and bring to a boil.
- Cook 1½ – 2 hours over medium heat to thicken. Do not cover. Stir often. Skim foam from top as needed.
- Ladle tomato mixture into hot quart jars.
- Process in boiling water bath.

Kary Foster Fettig

CARDWAL

Pickled Beets

MAKES 8-9 PINTS

For years, my mother, Beverly Foster, made her pickled beets from this, her mother's recipe. This recipe may be halved.

BEETS:
1/4 bushel beets
Water

- Wash beets well. Leave the root on and 1/2 inch of the top stem.
- "Size up" your beets, placing like-size beets in separate pans. (Larger beets will take longer to cook than smaller ones.)
- Add water to cover. Bring beets to boil and cook until slightly tender.
- Lift beets from pot and put in very cold water to loosen the skin.
- Peel beets.
- Slice or quarter the beets. Leave small beets whole.
- Put in sterile pint jars.

PICKLING SOLUTION:
2 cups white vinegar
2 cups water
2 cups sugar
1/2 teaspoon allspice
1/2 teaspoon whole cloves or 1/2 – 1 teaspoon ground cloves

- Bring the vinegar, water, sugar and spices to a rolling boil.
- Pour pickling solution over the beets, filling to 1/4 inch from the top.
- Process by boiling water bath method for 10 minutes.

Kary Foster Fettig

The Native American cemetery that was once on Wadsworth St. in Cross Village. The custom of the wreathes on the graves was aligned with the commemoration of All Saints Day on November first. The wreathes were decorated with streamers and crepe paper flowers in the favorite colors of the deceased, blessed in the church and placed on the crosses to replace the prior year's wreath. The wreathes "talked" in the wind and it was said the deceased wore and danced in them happy to be remembered.

Ethel's Beet Pickles

This recipe belonged to my mother-in-law, Ethel Fisher.

5 quarts small beets, cooked with 3-inch stems
3 cups vinegar
3 cups sugar
3 cups water in which the beets have been cooked
Stick of cinnamon, crushed
Whole cloves
Salt

- Bring vinegar, sugar and water to a boil.
- Add cooked beets and spices.
- Bring to boiling point. (I simmer for a little while.)
- Seal in sterilized jars.

Rosie Stolt

Cross Village, Mich.

Garden Corn Relish

2 pints corn, cut from cobs
1 quart ripe tomatoes, cut up
1 pint cucumbers, cut in small pieces
1 pint onions, diced
3 green peppers, diced

- Mix together.

BRINE:
1 pint vinegar
1 pint sugar
1 teaspoon celery seed
2 tablespoons salt

- Cook the brine for 1 hour.
- Pour over vegetables in sterilized pint jars.
- Scal and process.

Chris Krupa
Lieutenant, Firefighter and EMT Specialist
RFC Fire and Rescue Squad

Cranberry Relish

MAKES A LITTLE MORE THAN 1 QUART

Although many kitchens used to have food grinders, today's cooks might use a food processor for this relish.

4 cups (1 pound) cranberries
2 whole oranges
2½ cups sugar
1/2 teaspoon salt
Rind of an additional 1/2 orange

- Grind all together and put into sterilized jars.
- Process in hot water bath.

Carolyn Shear

Green Tomato Mincemeat

MAKES 5 PINTS

Use this sweet condiment like traditional mincemeat — in pies and cookies. Add a shot of brandy or rum to warmed mincemeat over ice cream. For openings at Three Pines Studio, I serve it as a wonderful accompaniment on crackers with Vermont white cheddar.

6 cups apples, peeled and chopped
6 cups green tomatoes, chopped
4 cups light brown sugar
1¼ cups cider vinegar
2 cups golden raisins
3 teaspoons ground cinnamon
1 teaspoon ground cloves
3/4 teaspoon ground allspice
3/4 teaspoon ground mace
2 teaspoons salt
1/2 teaspoon freshly ground pepper

- Mix apples and tomatoes together in a large pot. Add remaining ingredients.

- Bring gradually to a boil and simmer for 3 hours, stirring often.

- Spoon into clean, hot, sterilized jars, leaving 1/2 inch headspace. Seal.

- Process in boiling water bath for 25 minutes.

Joann Condino
Three Pines Studio, Cross Village

Nellie Bawkey's Raspberry Rhubarb Jam

MAKES 5 PINTS

Nellie always made at least a case of her jam for the Mini Fair bake sale.

10 cups rhubarb
6 cups sugar
4 3-ounce packages raspberry Jell-O gelatin
1 bottle Certo pectin

- Cut and freeze rhubarb. Thaw overnight.
- Sterilize jars.
- Bring rhubarb to boil, and then add sugar and Jell-O.
- Boil again on high. Turn off.
- Stir in 1 bottle of Certo pectin.
- Pour into sterilized jars, seal and process if desired.

Marge Edwards

Fall brings the celebration of the Pow-Wow or Homecoming Days in Cross Village.

Plum Butter – Powidla Sliwkowe

MAKES 16 PINTS OR 32 JELLY JARS

Use this wonderful fruit butter for pancakes, French toast, over ice cream with Grand Marnier and in desserts such as cobblers.

1/2 bushel plums
Water
4 cups sugar or less (If the fruit is very ripe, use less.)
1 teaspoon cinnamon or 1 cinnamon stick
1 vanilla bean, cut in half
1 tablespoon plus 1½ teaspoons lemon juice

- Halve plums. Remove pits.
- Put plums in a large pot. Add 1/4 cup water.
- Bring to boil. Turn the heat to simmer and cook until skins loosen, about 40 minutes, stirring frequently.
- At this point, you may put the whole mixture through a colander or food mill; or puree half of the mixture in a food processor.
- Put back in pan and add desired amount of sugar.
- Add 1 teaspoon of cinnamon or cinnamon stick, the vanilla bean cut in half and lemon juice.
- Continue simmering, stirring very often for 2 to 3 hours.
- It is done when it sticks to your wooden spoon.
- Remove cinnamon stick (if using) and vanilla bean.
- Sterilize jelly jars or pint jars and fill, seal and process in a hot water bath for 10 minutes.

Kary Foster Fettig

Cantaloupe Syrup

MAKES ABOUT 3½ PINTS

Cantaloupe syrup is delicious on pancakes, waffles, French toast and ice cream.

2 large very ripe cantaloupes (about 2½ pounds each), seeded, rind removed, cut into pieces
1½ quarts water
5 pounds sugar
½ cup fresh lemon juice
2 sticks cinnamon

- Puree the cantaloupe in a food processor or blender.
- Pour the purced cantaloupe into a large stock pot. Add 1½ quarts water to the puree. Heat to boiling. Reduce heat and simmer for 15 minutes.
- Add remaining ingredients. Simmer uncovered, stirring frequently, until mixture is the consistency of thick syrup, 1½ – 2 hours. Remove cinnamon.
- Pour into sterilized canning jars leaving 1/4 inch headspace in the jars.
- Process in a boiling water bath for 10 minutes.

Linda Little

Middle Village near Good Hart Mich.

A Heritage Recipe . . .

Raspberry Shrub

This fruit juice recipe was given to me in the 1970s by Bea Lamkin, known to her family as "Mom Bea." The shrub was brought up from the root cellar on special occasions. This recipe also makes a wonderful vinaigrette.

4 quarts raspberries, mashed
1 quart cider vinegar
3 – 4 cups of sugar for each quart of juice

- Put berries in a bowl. Cover them with vinegar.
- Cover the bowl and let stand overnight or 24 hours.
- Put the mixture in a "jelly bag" (a cloth bag made from cheesecloth, a tea towel or a cut-up sheet) and suspend it over a large bowl. Let the juice drip through.
- Squeeze the cloth, extracting all the juice.
- Measure juice.
- To each quart of juice add 3 – 4 cups of sugar.
- Boil the juice for 10 minutes and skim.
- Pour into sterilized jars and seal.
- Use 2 tablespoons of this mixture to 8 ounces of water or lemon-lime soda for an "old time" drink. The shrub can also be mixed with rum or brandy.

Ardyth Zeunen

Harbor Springs

Index

Index

Index

Index

Index

Index